W9-BXC-676

CLASSROOM DISCIPLINE

An Idea Handbook for Elementary School Teachers

CLASSROOM DISCIPLINE
An Idea Handbook for Elementary School Teachers

Dorothy McKellar Rogers

The Center for Applied Research in Education, Inc.
New York

The Center for Applied
Research in Education, Inc.
New York

Library of Congress
Catalog Card Number: 73-170727

Printed in the United States of America

C-1004-5

FOREWORD

Dissent and disruption have been rampant on college and high school campuses for the past decade. At Kent State, Jackson State, and Madison, real tragedies have occurred, tragedies which will not soon be forgotten. The Carnegie Commission on Higher Education commissioned a study and issued a report entitled *Dissent and Disruption.* Governmental commissions and committees have investigated and studied this phenomenon. Numerous books have been written on the subject.

Although there is much difference of opinion about the cause and effect relationship of campus disturbances, and even more difference of opinion about how to deal with the unrest and disruption, one fact has become eminently clear. Colleges do not know how to teach prospective teachers how to teach children about human rights. For whatever the reasons, we have failed miserably in this essential phase of education. The National Assessment Program sponsored by the Education Commission of the States has developed a substantial body of evidence to support this claim. The Phi Delta Kappa Teacher Education Project on Human Rights has corroborated the findings. Now the question is: "What are we going to do about it?" This book suggests several approaches.

Respect for individuality within any school system must be established at the top—by the board of education and the superintendent of schools. All board policy must reflect a recognition of each individual's worth, whether student, teacher, secretary, custodian, or administrator. Mutual trust between board, administration, and staff is dependent upon such policy and the integrity of the individuals who carry it out.

But well-conceived school board policy and people of integrity will not insure the development of mature, responsible individuals. Sensitive teachers who recognize and accept the individuality of each child are the key to a successful school experience—teachers who recognize and respect the human rights of children as people.

Even these teachers, however, need to acquire a number of specific skills and techniques. Although some of these skills may be intuitive, others can be learned through sharing the experiences of other teachers. That is what this book is all about. It is a compilation of some strategies and tactics used by some successful teachers to develop a classroom atmosphere conducive to learning for all—an atmosphere in which each individual's rights are respected and no person's opportunity to learn is sacrificed for the sake of the group.

When we have such an atmosphere, when we are teaching respect by example in the classroom throughout America—then and only then can we look for an end to the dissent and disruption which has rocked the campuses of America.

The reader is not expected to approve or accept all the suggestions offered. That an idea has worked for one teacher does not guarantee that it will work for another. Teaching, like learning, is a highly personal process. However, if the reader garners just two or three thoughts which will lead towards better classroom practice and observance of human rights, the effort has been justified.

Gregory C. Coffin,
Department of Instruction
Northeastern University
formerly
Superintendent of Schools
Evanston, Illinois

ABOUT THE AUTHOR

Dorothy McKellar Rogers has taught, tutored, and substituted in various Illinois schools at both the elementary and secondary levels. Her experience includes teaching in many different neighborhoods of Chicago and its environs. The ideas in this book are derived from her own teaching and from interviews with other teachers in the Evanston, Illinois, schools. These schools have a well-established reputation for excellence and serve a wide socioeconomic population span. The author of a number of articles and innovative ideas in professional publications, including *Grade Teacher* and *The Instructor,* Mrs. Rogers now teaches in the heart of a large eastern seaboard city.

Using This Handbook

This book can be used in a variety of ways.

Whatever our educational philosophy—whether we adopt this professor's premise or that scholar's thesis—the important point is that to carry it out in the classroom, we must have the necessary awareness and repertoire of ideas.

First, this book can be used as a reference guide. Let's say we're faced with a specific incident, e.g., stealing. As we read the section on stealing, the various ideas presented should stimulate our thinking to a solution which exactly fits the immediate situation.

Secondly, the book can be used as a polishing device. If we will choose a topic, such as "changing from one subject to another," and concentrate on improving transitions for at least a week, results are bound to appear. As we try various techniques, we can refine our style, and finally adopt the suggestions which are best for us.

Thirdly, the book can be used to plan a six-week campaign, let's say on better group discussions. We can incorporate suggestions from different portions of the book which apply to this problem. In this case we might find suitable material under Motivating Slow Students, Improving Discussion Techniques, and Correcting Work Habits.

Finally, let's consider the ideas in this book as guidelines and not as arbitrary rules. Teaching is a fine art. Every art has its own palette and brushes and the ideas in this book are for the art of teaching. Its aim is not to teach you to teach, but to allow you to teach.

DEALING WITH EVERYDAY INCIDENTS

Sometimes a tadpole, as Mark Twain would call him, does things "just cause"—like barefooting around town . . . skipping stones on water . . . sounding like a jay. It's a very wise reason and not to be tampered with. Most minor school incidents occur for a similar "just cause"; they are a natural part of growing up.

In our efforts to help students acquire self-control, we have reached an infusion-of-meaning mania; the universe, the king, and a royal tax rate are read into everyday happenings. Perhaps a little more humor, a little less anxiety, are needed. Since the overwhelming majority of behavior incidents are normal to growing up, we exhibit our normalcy, our genuine insight, by viewing them as normal rather than by trying to detect in the shadows the devious footsteps of Satan—or " . . . 'personality' is defined as an analytical constant, based on the observation of overt behavior which is consistent with the hypothesis that internal, systematically organized cognitions and affective relationships influence many overt behaviors in a relatively stable manner."

This book addresses itself to the normal: the normal classroom and its normal inhabitants, their problems, and how some of them have been solved. It includes several chapters on morale-building and concrete, proven ideas for promoting individual self-confidence and esprit de corps. It also provides several other chapters on mundane behavior problems, together with specific techniques which humane, excellent teachers are using with success in today's classrooms.

CREATING A GOOD CLASSROOM ATMOSPHERE

Discretion in choosing and applying the ideas in this book is the vital contribution of each individual teacher or user. Professional discernment will add the indefinable touch, the art, if you will, to creating and sustaining a good classroom atmosphere. Atmosphere is the essence of a natural classroom control, and the right blend of components for an outstanding atmosphere is difficult to convey. A superb teacher may comment simply, "Discipline is not a real problem," without analyzing it further. The personality which enables a teacher to find authentic rapport with young people is modest; she is unlikely to consider herself enough of an authority to write a book on the subject. Yet such teachers have made this book possible. I am very grateful for their generous contributions of time and advice.

My primary purpose in writing this handbook, which is meant to be kept on a teacher's desk, is to help her stimulate her thinking and imagination at the crucial times she needs answers. Confronted with youngsters' impulsive antics and problems, the classroom teacher encounters her "teachable moments" daily. Every suggestion contained in this book has been offered by a practicing, gifted teacher. Many teachers have never had a good course in classroom control; or if they had one, it was many moons ago. This book can close that gap.

From the variety of proven answers which are offered for each problem, a teacher's imagination may weave clever composites to meet her immediate requirements. Better still, they may prompt her to discover her own unique solutions. Certainly, the given examples can be successfully copied, per se, if the approach fits the individual teacher's predicament and personality.

Dorothy McKellar Rogers

ACKNOWLEDGMENTS

I wish to thank the following teachers and educators who were generous in sharing their experience and ideas with the author.

Contributors of Ideas. Jerry Abern, Helene Abernathy, Michele Abrams, Ron Amend, Corene Anderson, Elizabeth Arras, Leo Benson, Ann Bevan, Kathryn Blair, Charlotte Bond, Marjorie Bredehorn, Judith Brostoff, Jean Buck, Elise Burkholder, Norma Core, Yvonne Davis, Eddie M. Ellis, Kathryn English, James Elliot, Betty Fisher, Clara Floyd, Mary Flynn, Edith Ford, Barbara Friedberg, Cathy Freeman, Martha Gauger, Ronald Gearing, Jackie Gerth, Bonnie Billespie, Ethel Grays, Betty Hall, Mary Hunter, Barbara Huntzicler, Lyn Hyndman, Mary Jenkins, Irene Kantner, Wendy Klein, Jean Kixmiller,

Myril Landsman, Edna Lehman, Mary Lenahan, Caroline Lewis, June Marquette, Hester Meeder, Marilee Mercer, Eleanor Metzger, Charlotte Meyer, Virginia Milne, Dorothy M. Muldoon, Eunice Neal, Helen Newell, Avian O'Connor, Edward O'Reilly, Edward Pearson, Margaret Payne,

Alita Reicin, Bessie M. Rhodes, Anne Richter, Judy Ritter, Ernest Robbins, Liam Roomey, Edna Saewart, Gary Sanders, Ruth Ann Sayre, Judy Segal, Trudy Selz, Joy Simon, Edward Smail, Janet Smucker, Irene Spensley, Candas Sullivan,

Charles Thomas, Jean Thorsen, Stuart Vincent, Sarah Weingarten, Mildred Werner, Susan Wheeler, Carol Wilkinson, Alice Wimberly, Carol Yoder . . . and to the many, many others who shared their ideas with me in more informal moments in the teacher's lounge, at the lunch table, and sometimes even at teachers' meetings. I wish I had written down your names; I certainly remembered your ideas.

CONTENTS

1 Increasing Desire to Attend School

How does a child feel about the classroom, really? For most children it is a home away from home.

The word home means different things to different people. Some think of it as "the dearest place on earth," some as a haven, and others as a base for operations. If we think of a classroom serving as another home, what must it offer—as the second dearest place on earth?

Certainly, one of the child's basic needs, a genuine place in the group, must be firmly established as an assured fact. Each pupil must feel the power which exists in warm and lasting relationships with associates who believe in him. Everyone is responsible for treating others consistently, courteously, and honestly. In addition to teaching solid moral values and their application to self-control, this second home must also help the child establish worthwhile goals for which *he* wants to work.

The classroom as a haven? It can be a refuge from the limitations which ignorance and the ignorant would place on many individuals. It should be a sanctuary from the character shriveling influence of frightening authoritarianism on one hand and aimless apathy on the other. A place of refuge is the best spot to dissipate the illusion that life has a magic carpet ride to success. Life offers something far better than downhill roads to the top.

The classroom as a base of operations? Out of today tomorrow is built, so the qualities of curosity and imagination must be coupled with systematic training in productive work approaches. Work can be very enjoyable. The child must have help in the intelligent use of his time; time must be a servant, not a master of actions.

Happily, the school room can be a combination of all three elements of home: a dear place on earth, a haven and a base of operations. The following sections contain comments on basic ideas, suggestions, and techniques by which teachers can make each child feel more at home.

Roll Call

What could be kinder than to let a child know you really care? Yet you must be sincere in your expressions of interest, fair in the amount of time devoted to each pupil, and consistent from day to day. One approach which is sure to include everyone is to make roll call more personal. The child immediately recognizes that you see him as individual when, for example, you ask him about his likes and dislikes.

More than a name in her book

Call roll. Each child answers with "present" and a fact about himself. One day ask for his middle name; another time, a well liked movie, or a favorite hobby, a pet's name, a favorite dinner. The last one strikes an especially responsive chord in children.

A variation: Make a list of 8 or 10 TV programs popular with the age group. Call roll. Ask each child to answer with the name of his favorite show. A student helper keeps tally. Announce results. Children love this, and it's a splendid step toward building an "our room" feeling.

Picture, picture on the wall

Place each child's picture over his locker or coat hook. Now he can't miss putting his coat and hat in the right place. If you take the pictures, pose several youngsters in one exposure, cut and mount separately.

That's me . . . . . . over there

Let each child draw a self portrait, perhaps using a mirror. Put child's name and birthday on completed drawing. Hang pictures low—under a chalk board ledge, for example. Assign a child to take roll by turning over pictures of absent children.

Importance of the Individual—Respect

As you think it over, you'll probably agree that it's hard to dislike or resent anyone whom you know respects you greatly. Often it's easy to like someone whom we consider less fortunate or inferior; weaknesses often make others seem loveable—but it's harder to love someone we consider our superior. At the same time it's easy to respect our superiors and more difficult to respect those under us. Indeed, we must be particularly careful to respect individuals whom we are asked to teach and criticize. If we want the healthiest relationship with them, they must know that we respect them.

That's all she wrote

When sending a note home with a non-reading child, please read the contents to him before asking him to carry it. It dissolves his fear of the message. Certainly, it is respectful of his feelings, and a courteous thing to do.

Private Property . . . No Trespassing

Your example establishes the tone of respecting privacy and property rights of others. Ask your student, "May I look into your desk?"

At your convenience, sir

You have a reasonable doubt about a child's guilt in an incident. Still, you must question him. Please be sure to ask him, "When would it be convenient for you to talk to me?"

My lens is better than yours

If a stupid act requires reproof, be sure to let the culprit know you have a better concept of him than he has of himself. Example: "I really thought you were a man here . . . the one character who kept his cool." Or: "Of all the kids around, I really didn't expect this of you." (But don't say this if you don't feel it's true.)

Buck up, buddy boy

Patting a young boy on the back is a token of friendship. As you do, add a few warm words. Many successful teachers told me the importance of physical touching of the child in a casual way. Please be careful—a pat on the top of the head is patronizing, a pat on the arm or back is reassuring.

Importance of Individual—Equality (No One Is More Equal)

Each child is as important to the class as an individual facet is to a diamond. His uniqueness and his equality can be brought out, sometimes simultaneously. In recent years strong emphasis has been placed on racial equality, and we are slowly awakening to our obligations to the minorities. However other aspects of equality are important, too. We must guard against allowing IQ test scores to promote an intellectual aristocracy and an intellectual peonage. Constantly we must work on fairness in personal relationships. We must work on giving opportunities which are fair. Our concern for equality must go beyond civil rights, intellectual rights, and on to include personal, property and social rights.

My teacher likes everybody

Each day show your affection for each child. Make a personal comment to him. At first you may have to use a check sheet to be sure you've missed no one.

Everybody's name is important

If any student were teacher, he'd need to know the name of each person in the class. During the first week of school assign this task. Every child must learn every other person's name, first and last. A bingo card approach is one method.

One class of citizens

Constantly we are told to show equality of opportunity: here it is in action. Arrange math groups according to individual progress but eliminate pigeonholing by allowing for genuine flexibility. Insist each child sit with his assigned group for the presentation. Then allow him to sit in on any other group he chooses. He won't get all that's offered, but he will learn something. Generally, children choose rather well: those most ready for promotion to a better section are the most grateful.

Birthday celebrations

Notice sent to parents:

When the school or even a classroom takes a definite stand on keeping birthday parties and school separate, it circumvents many hidden hurts among children. Explain to the parents that each birthday child is honored by a song, poem, birthday wishes and a birthday badge. That's all. No special cookies or treats are brought to school, no party invitations are to be distributed at school, and party gifts and favors are not to be brought to school after home parties.

Save those extra shekels

Halloween costumes need not be more expense for parents. Set the tone for wise economy by sending a note home expressing a school viewpoint. It helps each child accept his parents' decision more completely.

Oakton School

Dear Parents,

On Thursday, October 31st, the children may wear Halloween costumes to school. Please do not feel obligated to buy a costume especially for this day. A piece of old sheet makes a ghost, or it's fun to dress up in long skirts, old blouses, hats, pants, belts, scarves, jewelry or cowboy suits.

Your child is to wear his costume to school. For your child's protection and comfort, NO MASKS WILL BE WORN IN SCHOOL OR TO AND FROM SCHOOL. Harmless makeup is fine, and more fun too.

Thank you for your cooperation.

Happy Halloween.

Every lad and lassie is a wee different

An Interest Inventory given monthly shows a child his uniqueness. It carries an added advantage of stimulating him to pinpoint his interest inclinations. The form on page 24 is a good example.

Importance of Individual—Children With Problems

This section contains a few ideas on how to make life more liveable for the troubled child and the teacher. Often the very children who make you feel you could hardly care less about them, desperately need you to care. Expert counseling is the answer, but it isn't always available when you need it, and sometimes it's just humanly impossible for the classroom teacher to take the necessary time, even if she has the qualifications of an expert. This section is not intended to impinge on the activities of specialists in counseling. However, troubled children often respond well to patient, informal counseling, and disruptive antics will just fade away . . . sometimes.

INTEREST INVENTORY

1. At school, what I like to do best is ______________________
2. At home, what I like to do best is ______________________
3. What I like least at school is ______________________
4. What I like least at home is ______________________
5. I would like to study more about ______________________
6. I don't want to study any more about ______________________
7. When I grow up I'd like to be ______________________
8. The most interesting things I remember doing in school were ______________________
9. The happiest day I remember was ______________________
10. The things I try to save are ______________________
11. My favorite sports or games are ______________________
12. I know I need more help to ______________________
13. The kinds of books I like to read best are ______________________
14. If I could travel anywhere in the world, I would like to go to ______________________
15. In my spare time I like to ______________________

As your friend and teacher, I care

Early assure everyone he *can* pass. You do care and because you care, you'll insist that each child do a certain amount of work. Eliminate all general threats of flunking.

Troublemaking Tommy

First thing in the morning, greet him with a compliment about something which he has done right. No act is too small to be mentioned.

. . . . . Leave your troubles behind

You see a child in a bad mood coming through the door. Immediately give him a special responsibility: moving books, passing papers, posting a bulletin. It'll help him get into the swing of the school day and leave his worries at the door.

One dog house is enough

A problem child is well aware of his temporary outcast status when he's been sent back from gym or library. Don't scold. Be a friend first. As an equal talk about anything he wants to talk about.

Breaking bread together

You have a hard-to-reach or problem child. Ask him to lunch with you in the classroom. Make it one day a week for several weeks. While conversing, work on developing friendship. Don't try for an attitude change, or to convert him to what you regard as the good life.

Dear red box . . . my problem is

Use a red file box for children's notes. If they would like more friends, learn how to deal with a demanding younger sister, or what have you, ask them to leave a note in the box. Later, the group discusses all problems and offers solutions. A 20 minute period once a week covers nicely.

A special pal

A special interest project for the 1½ percent or 2 percent hard core behavior problems: Social worker and teacher jointly decide a specific pupil-teacher friendship assignment for each member of the staff. Social worker helps each teacher decide on a loose pattern of activity for each case. No teacher is assigned to one of his own pupils; thus a child has a faculty friend who is not his boss. No teacher is given more than one problem child to be a buddy to.

Importance of Individual–Shyness

Charming as it may seem, shyness stems from egocentric fear. Naturally, the long term improvement program for curing shyness includes overcoming fear, building self-confidence, developing skills, etc., while the immediate steps involve encouraging the child to forget about himself and think about others. Perhaps he'll be set to work on special projects. Some of the following suggestions are excellent for teaching over-quiet children to be more outgoing.

Let your puppets do the talking

Give the child a puppet and take one yourself. Start a conversation between the puppets. Always make the youngster ask the questions. Then let the child's puppet continue to ask the questions while you give answers without using a puppet. When the child seems to feel at home with his puppet, encourage him to talk with a few children, using his puppet.

Warm as a puppy's welcome

A new enrollee joins the class. Choose two friendly welcomers. Pick children who were new last year, if possible. If selection permits, choose one who arrived shy and the other one who was always self-assured. Have a meeting. Explain: The newest arrival is shy and needs special friendship acts. Ask your once-shy helper to remember how he felt when he first came to this school. He is to help from that standpoint. Ask the poised one to remember what he did to make an easy adjustment.

Play partners day

Each child chooses a partner for this entire red letter day. Quietly suggest to your shy one, "Choose the child in the room you most want to be like." Almost invariably the shy child will choose a very out-going youngster.

"Fresh thoughts dressed in warm words"

Daily call the shy child to your desk and have a short conversation. Talk can be of many things. Continue these rendezvous for several weeks before you attempt an evaluation.

Speak out, little fellow

Let a shy child look like a leader. Send him on errands to the office or other rooms. Give him oral, not written messages. Tell a close teacher friend what you're doing and ask her to lengthen her conversations with the chap.

Scuttling the shyness shakes

A child too shy to read? Take her separately and ask her to whisper the reading words. Tell her you'll work together daily. Each time you expect her to whisper a little louder and clearer. Set a goal of two weeks for her to surprise her reading group. Count off the days for her; seven more, six more, five more days.

MAKING SCHOOL MORE DELIGHTFUL

A senior/junior partner concept of the teacher-student relationship is in step with present day standards. In this kind of mental setting it's natural to genuinely expect good attitudes, bright actions and happy results. The senior partner is less tempted to "set kids right." Any junior partner is recognized as having full potential, and he is expected to grow in personality, responsibility, and capability.

We all need to feel that we fit into the picture, that we are wanted and are where the action is. Your first step is to find (and stay in) the position where you feel needed and your talents are appreciated. This move is vital to setting the right tone: more than your well-being is at stake. When you've identified the place that's right for you, you stand in the strongest position to help students intelligently.

Include, include, include. Attraction is based on being included. If you would attract children to school, include them not only overtly in daily action but also silently in daily thinking. This means that every child is an integral part of your class, which has no appendages called behavior problems. Every member of your class belongs with you. Not one is merely assigned to your room.

If you'd attract children to learning, don't exclude yourself from the role of learning. Be a learner along with them. Though timing can be tricky, mechanics of teaching are rather simple. The heart and soul of teaching, a real challenge, too, is learning to combine mellowness of attitude with exhilarating expectations regarding student capabilities and interests.

Some very charming teachers offered these techniques for adding zest to the school day, and in a few cases add glee to the scene.

Harry and Whiskers

Impersonalize and dramatize school and class rules by using puppets to explain them. Puppets appeal to children's imagination and playfulness. Have puppets talk into your ear and relay the information.

Example: Harry and Whiskers have lived in room 103 for so long they know all the rules. In summer they stay under a counter in a big box. In September, when boys and girls arrive, the puppets get to live on top of the counter. This makes them glad.

Harry is very shy, so he whispers into teacher's ear. He asks her lots of questions, too. He keeps wanting to know *why* some rules exist. Whiskers has a serious physical weakness: noise hurts his ears.

"Ask not for whom the bell tolls . . ."

In the morning ring a small bell as a signal for everyone to start working. Use the bell to shift from one activity to another all day. Ring it sparingly for special announcements, but avoid using it to quiet the class. Also, you might want to let a different child do the actual ringing each day. He would rely on your cues.

Freeze

This has enjoyed immense popularity because the children consider it fun. When you need the class's attention, call out "Freeze." Everyone stops as if hit by a freeze gun ray. Speak your piece, and then command, "Unfreeze," to get the action going again.

Minutemen to the rescue

Tell class stories of the original minutemen. Today's minutemen are teacher's helpers, ready on a moment's notice to carry out special tasks and errands in minutes. Youngsters arrive back huffing and puffing but very proud of themselves.

It's a two way street

Return at least one set of graded papers daily. Younsters turn in their work daily. Show them, don't merely tell them, that you're doing your part. Collect papers again and save them for a weekly folder if you like.

"Happy as a clam at high water"

Establish free periods twice a day. Elicit 20 or 25 ideas from the children of possible activities. Discuss briefly why some of the other suggestions can't be included. Ditto and distribute the list. Schedule free time, about ten minutes in the morning and 20 minutes in the afternoon. The morning period can come anytime after work has been completed; however, in the AM children work alone. For the afternoon block off a definite period, say 2:00 to 2:20. During this time, a child may work alone or with another, as he prefers.

Favorite subject? "creativity"

Early in the morning, while children are fresh, have a creativity period. Each day, that is. You'll find this period should last about 30 to 40 minutes. But be flexible here, play it by ear. You'll sense when activities become aimless or listless.

For smooth operating have paints, papers, games, records, books, film strips all available. At first you may have to circulate among students, suggesting activities. Children need natural, gradual training on using various facilities and on learning to respond to their imaginative impulses. Give the entire project a trial of several weeks before trying to evaluate it.

Black Jack

A great way to re-enforce addition facts: Teach children the card game called Black Jack. You won't have to coax them to study.

Sneak preview

If a children's classic is coming soon on TV, scoop the video world. Introduce the story, perhaps reading a portion aloud, or holding a group discussion. Suggest highlights and details to watch for.

Bookworms? . . . . . a whole can of them

One worm's head per classmate. A worm grows a segment for each book read. Naturally, the easiest place to keep this many worms is in a large can. Let each child make his own worm's head of construction paper, put his name on the back of it, and later he can make segments as he needs them. Title of a book goes on the back of each segment.

Diagnostic, no. Effective, yes

In the fall let children choose their initial reading texts. Surprisingly, between 60 percent and 75 percent of your children will select the level at which they should be working. Others readily accept your suggested changes.

Example: First, put in a few words on using good judgment. Then, 1) Place many readers on a table. If you have a 3rd grade, put out easy and difficult 2nd, 3rd, and 4th grade texts. 2) Send one row of students to the table at a time.

Land, sea, or air

Name reading-groups after animals or birds, but with a new flair. Select creatures which move in unusual ways. Let children go to reading group in that fashion. Ducks waddle. Lions stalk. Bunnies hop. Turtles bobble their heads. Don't be afraid this will cause commotion in the room. It doesn't have to. Instead, it can ease the atmosphere.

Chattering teeth or chattering children

Have a warm heart. Let children eat and play in the room in extreme weather. One rule: If children elect to eat in room, they may leave only for washroom or for a drink. No frolicking in halls. And no changing their minds and going outside.

CONCLUSION

Home is where the heart is, and the heart yearns to be where it feels at home. Warmth, protection and a sure foundation stone are essential factors in both a home and a classroom. In these places the importance of the individual should be stressed and consequently he should be shown how to bring his uniqueness to light. Belonging is first. His name is on the roster; now you need more information of the sort *he* considers important. He's respected. His rights as well as his group responsibilities are of immediate concern.

He's an equal to anyone. As you bring out his native quality in fullness, thoughts of inequality will begin to fade. Like the different facets of a diamond, each child catches light in his own way. He can't take anyone else's light. His presence adds depth and luster to the whole.

Personal problems. The cramping effect of shyness has plagued almost everyone at one time or another. Since quietness accompanies shyness, the greatest danger is overlooking it or dismissing it with the thought that, "he'll outgrow it."

When informally counseling students, try to center discussions on general problems and conditions and then simply show the child how his problems merely fit into the whole. If attention is focused on what his teacher or classmates think of his problems, the student may feel overwhelmed and isolated.

Enchantment is normal. Adding, when least expected, mirth and enchanting surprises to the school day gives a charm and buoyancy. Blended with hard work, the results yield a flourishing learning atmosphere.

2 Improving Communication and Committees

Silence, thoughful silence, is the first requirement for the "feast of reason and the flow of soul" (Pope) which makes for richness in conversation and discussion. Brevity and restraint on the teacher's part reflects effective disciplining and marshaling of her thinking. Good teachers listen, and listen again to their own better judgment, before they speak.

Progressively mounting footsteps show yesterday's best as not good enough for today's best. We know a great deal about expected avenues for children's growth. What path into the golden sunrise of learning are we taking for ourselves? Basically we command our subject matter and are aware of good instructional methods. Constantly trying to improve our tact and succinctness in communication keeps us in a daily growth pattern essential to fine teaching. This sense of progress will protect our early enthusiasm, and it will help us avoid the pitfall common to many splendid, experienced teachers—going to seed.

No espionage system ever devised has outclassed the underground communications network which youngsters set up intuitively when danger threatens their common good. Not a word spoken, but the message spreads. So we don't have to teach them to communicate: we have to teach them how to reach us in a form we understand, at our present level of interest.

Distinct communication problems are taken up elsewhere. This chapter addresses itself only to promoting the flow and exchange of ideas. Even the present discussion is confined to several elements which are of focal interest only to the practicing teacher: controlled whispering, class discussion, informal and formal group techniques, individual constructive protest, and finally, some good suggestions and plans for committees.

CONTROLLED WHISPERING

No one need explain the advantages of allowing children the freedom of talking quietly among themselves. An easy working atmosphere does all that educators claim for it, but children need to feel a background stability.

First, decide the best decibel level for your room. Second, *expect to systematically train* children into accepting this level. This is far better than correcting or scolding them into it. Use short, specific lessons or training periods. Third, set up a student monitor arrangment, both for self-government benefits and to relieve you of holding the line. Finally, for the sake of your balanced outlook as well as their encouragement, express appreciation, silently and aloud, for notches of improvement in individual and group self-control.

From time to time you'll be faced with a need for review training sessions, but don't take this too much to heart. You know well that even in all-adult groups the chairman must sometimes call for, "Order, order."

Here are some excellent, proven techniques which some widely admired teachers have successfully employed.

Whisper, whisper–a game

Children need practice in learning to modulate their voices. Start with four training sessions of five to ten minutes each over a period of two weeks. Repeat later in the year if the original lessons seem to have faded.

Directions: Children mingle and whisper to others. If you or one chosen person can hear what they are saying, they must drop out of the game, go to one side of the room and stand patiently.

Stage whisper–real whisper

Give examples of each and define the terms. Ask them if they ever heard of stage whisper before. Then every day for two weeks have them practice five minutes of whispering into each other's ears.

Monkey see, monkey do

Stand close to noisy children and whisper when you correct them for loud talking. Tell them they are to use the same volume you are using. A teacher who stands catty-corner and calls, "Be quiet, Joshua," adds considerably to the noise herself and simultaneously sets a bad example.

Is that a flea in my ear?

Make a loud SSSSS sound. Explain how whispering at a distance sounds almost like that. If you, as teacher, can't hear anything more of what the children are saying than SSSSSS, they're not talking too loudly.

Soft as a morning breeze in the leaves

Desks touching one another reduce children's desire to talk. Yet, when they really need to converse, they can keep their voices very low. Group the desks in clusters of two or four. Consider students' personalities, and work for complements: quiet/noisy, dawdling/diligent, quick/slow learners.

We take care of our own, thank you

Arrange children's desks in clusters of eight. One child in each group acts as a monitor during homeroom and free periods. Children like this way as they seem to be more amenable to quiet requests from another child than from an adult.

Change the challenge . . . . . change the chair

Different seat assignments for different types of lessons crystalize an understanding of the degree of conversing permitted in each. Have one seating chart for lab work or committee sessions, and another for lecture and silent reading sessions. If you have two sets of chairs, better still.

Stop . . . proceed with caution . . . go

This noise level device is effective when basic control of the class has been established. Use three paper strips: red, yellow, green. Red means no talking. Yellow means discreet communication such as asking the next child for an eraser, or a question.

Green means general quiet conversation. Mount the strip conspicuously on your desk or on a bulletin board. Yellow is used most of the time.

Take two . . . . . .

Turn off the lights, a signal that everyone may stop working and have a talk-time break. Allow quiet chatter for a minute or two, never more than three. Switch lights on for a return to business as usual. In some cases tell your principal ahead of time; your room might seem disorderly to him should he stroll past.

Trooping the colors

A class needs to be trained into a sense of appropriateness concerning whispering in the room, or when to leave seats. The following technique is an excellent transition step from a teacher-controlled classroom to a self-directed one. After almost everyone has had a turn at being a messenger, the class will understand the rules well. After the children are sure of what's expected of them as a group, you can eliminate the yellow card entirely and each child can bring his own red card to your desk.

Directions: 1) Create the post of room messenger. This heady station in life is shared on a scheduled basis. 2) Issue two colored cards to each student–say, yellow and red. 3) Students hold up yellow cards to signal messenger for a pencil sharpening job, dictionaries, maps, ditto sheets, etc. Students hold up red card when they want the teacher's help. The red cards have row and seat numbers or student names. The messenger leaves cards at your desk, and you are to help as soon as convenient. In the meantime students are relieved of time-wasting holding-up-the-hand, and are free to return to the pursuit of knowledge, etc.

10 . . . 9 . . . 8 . . . 7 . . .

Often when introducing this a teacher hears, "Gee, that's fair," or, "Fair enough," from some young voices. It's a great device for training children into the whispering level best for good working conditions. Normally, children enjoy this challenge of numbers and it seems to shift focus away from the teacher herself.

Example: During a time when youngsters are doing seat work, committee planning, or working on projects, and are getting too noisy–stop all activity. Tell them they're too boisterous and you're going to have a count-down. Put a ten on the board.

Explain that they may converse quietly but everytime you must check the entire class, a small group, an individual, or if there's an unidentified cat-call, you'll simply lower the number. If the number reaches zero, you'll have your own blast-off and in the process they'll lose a special movie, a gym or whatever. If it's a treat the class wants badly, they'll do a splendid job of monitoring each other.

You did it once, you can do it again

When pupils are working at a satisfactory noise level, tell them so. Compliment them mildly. CAUTION: Compliment them simply and matter-or-factly, so they'll continue at the same pace. If you praise their quietness profusely, they overreact, and everyone starts talking. Sometimes, when the group is a little noisy, tell them, "Tuesday, you were perfect in holding a good level of talking. Let's go back to it."

As you can see, the common thread in each of these methods is two-ply: first, reasonable expectations of the children; and second, explicit standards.

HANDLING CLASS AND GROUP DISCUSSION

"Silver tongues and airy phrases" delightfully describes much that passes for thoughtful classroom discussion. Beyond content, other aspects which need improvement are the total percentage of active participants and the length of time during which they are really interested in the proceedings. No facet of teaching is easier to do in a mediocre fashion or harder to do really well.

Discussion time claims to be communication time, and good communication requires three fundamental elements. The first is *understanding*–understanding the facts being presented and the background and attitudes of those being addressed. True communication requires a giver and a receiver. The second is appropriate *vocabulary,* understood and accepted by both sides. The third essential is *sincerity,* the honesty of straight thinking and speaking. Children feel sincerity.

The pivot point in the art of discussion is individual questions, intuitively worded. Usually, of course, you'll start your questions on specific vivid topics and lead into deeper meanings. Later, when you want to emphasize a point, or summarize, raise your voice a bit. Better still, lower it noticeably.

One exceptional social studies teacher has developed a three-level question technique for his heterogeneous classes. Reading assignments are in different source materials. He prepares a list of three question types, A, B, and C. To the slow student he addresses a question on fact: When and where did the Civil War start? To the average student he addresses a question involving simple thought: Why do you think it started at Fort Sumter? And to the serious student he addresses a question or underlying pattern: Why were both sides so trigger-happy?

Thus poor readers can close the gap somewhat by learning to listen very attentively. Class notes are extremely important, since test questions are taken from discussions rather than readings. Of course, this takes lots of careful teacher preparation. Freedom to amble around the mental countryside is somewhat curtailed, but it's a splendid way to lead most students into the pastureland of active participation.

As a professional, you sense when to stick to the script and when to ad-lib. Even so, unstructured discussions don't always unfold intelligently. They may just get floppy. When a student conducts a discussion, be sure he has a central theme and a prepared reservoir of questions and provocative comments. Whether he follows it, or uses his own purposeful plan, is of secondary importance. Having done his homework, as they say in political circles, he feels more self-confidence. He knows where he is going. Responses from the group are always better.

A review of a few guidelines in the methods and art of class discussion:

1. Lead from the known into the unknown.
2. Use lively illustrations and examples, lots of them.
3. Center discussion among the students, if they're sincerely thinking about the material.
4. Really welcome good answers beyond the one you had in mind.

Individual teachers regard the following informative suggestions as valuable aids:

Mystery and suspense . . . . . . who's next?

Add a sharpness which no teacher's choice could bring by letting the first student choose the next to recite, read aloud, or answer a question. The students' responsibility in calling the order encourages them to keep the place in a reading group or while correcting math papers. Unruly classes respond well. Younger children delight in it. A success, always, and you can readily see why: it capitalizes on the children's natural interest in each other.

Directions: Establish these ground rules: 1. A boy calls on a girl and a girl must call on a boy; children are usually shy about being the first to make the cross-over between sexes. 2. Ask each child to select two or three names to call on ahead of time: this eliminates the hemming and hawing which causes the activity to lose tempo. 3. Every child has a first turn before anyone has a second.

The bloke keeps blurting out

When a student persists in speaking out of turn during a class discussion, don't scold. It ruins the free flowing atmosphere you're trying to build. Don't let him ruin the discussion, either. Try, "Jim, please learn to raise your hand," and in the same breath, "George, would you give us the answer?" Calmly and casually said, the switch illustrates that self-control is the order of the day. Repeat this a number of times, and the class will respond well.

Help him out of the corner

Ask a fumbling student, "Would you choose someone in the room to help you with the answer?"

A baker's dozen

12 to 14 is a good number of students for incisive, nimble discussion. Several shorter sessions with this number yield more than a long discussion with the whole class. (That is, other things being equal.) Seat your student friends in the most primitive communal form, a circle. Around a round table is even better.

He may not always be right . . . . .

But hardly ever tell a student bluntly, "You're wrong." Instead, comment, "That's close," or "You're on the right track." For an impossible answer, "That's an observation I hadn't thought of."

FORMAL GROUP DISCUSSION

True group discussion is a miniature seminar. It compares with aimless, half-baked class discussion as a mountain lake at sunrise compares with a stone quarry pond. The basic elements are the same—a hole full of water, sun and a breeze. The tarn has fresh water and depth; oblique light rays sparkle the rippling; and usually this is set among evergreens. Likewise, well prepared discussion has depth, springing, lively ideas, sparkling insights in constantly shimmering change as members contribute from a rich background.

Conversation often is most appealing in its most spontaneous moments, but then, generally, conversation is informal communication with informal or very immediate goals. The old-fashioned classroom recitation, question rack and prescribed answers, is at the other pole. Modern class discussion must draw from both if it's going to be outstanding. Some established information and ideas, facts and findings, must be blended with fluent expression of the participants' opinions if they're going to grow into new insights on the subject.

Youngsters love immediacy. "Let's have a discussion, right now." Sometimes it's not bad, other times they merely rehash limited expressions on a subject. But if you can hold out and tactfully insist on their preparing the soil, they may never thank you because they may never recognize just why the discussion was better, a lot better.

Discussion Dynamics

An elementary definition of group discussion is problem solving by several people talking and thinking together. It is not rambling conversation. Every good discussion has some basic characteristics:

1. It must include everyone present.
2. The fundamental factor is a common problem, and the talkers must be interested in a solution.
3. Participants must be informed with facts, general information and ideas.
4. It is based on objective thinking toward the problem, the participants, and one's own ideas.
5. Thinking should follow the pattern of define, analyze, examine, evaluate.
6. Always, the group leader must remember he's the chairman.
7. Good listening is necessary.

This basic pattern applies at any age level. Does it seem too heady for your young students? It really isn't.

At any age, a leader of group discussion, either teacher or student, has special responsibilities. First, he must clarify the objective . . . . What is it we want to get out of this discussion? Although the leader may not announce it, he has mentally worked out essential ideas in a logical order. And finally, his concluding remarks should reinforce in the minds of everyone what has gone on, and some of the ideas they should have garnered from it.

Even genius needs a guideline

Pass out the following form and let the pupils examine it. Perhaps you'll even want to go over some points with them. They have the scheduled group discussion. Afterwards have the class fill in the evaluation sheet.

Discussion Evaluation Sheet

	Yes	No
1. Was there an attempt to focus the discussion on a problem?		
2. Did leader end discussion with a concluding summary or remark?		
3. Was an attempt made to draw most of the group into the discussion?		
4. Do you feel you did your share in participating in the discussion?		
5. Did you get anything out of it?		

6. How would you rate the discussion in terms of the standards we have set up? Circle the number which tells your view. (Number 5 represents the highest score.)

5 4 3 2 1

Further comments or suggestions

An old, old chestnut

But it works. Explain to students beforehand—you'll speak to disruptive characters once or twice. No more. After that, if you must speak to anyone for being distractive, you'll write his name on a card and you'll reckon with him later. If it's natural and convenient take the blank card to the student's desk and let him watch you write his name. Why it's more effective this way, I don't know, but it is. Most often a student will shape up for the rest of the period after his name has been written down. If he has made valid contributions in the interim, why not let him go without a scolding?

TEACHING CONSTRUCTIVE PROTEST

Little children protest. They yowl. Bigger ones bite. Then it's away to school, and there we often neglect to show them suitable ways to protest against abuses, or seeming abuses of adult power. School power. School authorities are few in number but from the child's viewpoint they have vast privilege. Sometimes the privilege is abused.

All students need safety valves. If children have no release, nor voice, they develop a burdened feeling of resentment which we call oppression. Four typical reactions to oppression are: 1) Apathy; 2) Hostility; 3) Conforming and voicing objection; 4) Confrontation. Many of you already know more about confrontation than I do, and the subject of hostility has been ably covered by other authors. Since apathy comes from the oppression of the spirit, it indicates the most severe reaction and the greatest feeling of hopelessness. Many times it's far more dangerous than confrontation because it's more deadly and self-defeating.

In most circumstances, conforming and voicing objections courteously is the most reasonable and mature reaction. It is a learned skill; it involves developing traits of self-assurance, patience and perspicacious persistence. Seeing home examples, or hearing parents who use this approach when discussing incidents helps boys and girls acquire a sense of touch and timing. Obviously, if a child comes from a one-parent home, he overhears fewer adult conversations and reasoning. Usually the one parent must perform household duties like getting dinner, and so hasn't the time to converse and reason with the child as much as she might like to.

Someone must teach children how to object intelligently, since the grooming of tomorrow's reasonable protesters starts today. Children learn gradually how to disagree with authority courteously. Disagreement without letting tempers flare is a fine art, even for adults.

Usually, when interviewing teachers for this book, I talked to them in their classrooms. So I had the advantage of being exposed to the general feel of each room. From this background I submit the following as being some of the best suggestions I heard on the subject of constructive protest.

Sorry, that's not quite right

Make mistakes with obvious facts. Misread the clock. Call children's names wrongly. Turn off the lights at the wrong time. Give a story the wrong ending. Automatically, the children will correct you. Choose the most pleasant or tactful correction and discuss it with the class.

Better than a voodoo doll for practice

Carefully choose a target topic. It must be debatable, of peak interest, and not too emotionally charged: bedtimes—weekend curfew—make-up—ball teams. Structure a practice session using role-playing. Additional practice: Let a child take his parents' viewpoints and support them, especially if the child disagrees with his parents.

In my considered opinion

Ask the children to write you a letter when they feel you have been unfair. It may take several invitations on your part before they feel free to do it. Make it very clear that the writer will not jeopardize his relationship with you by expressing his feelings honestly. Signed letters are much preferred, but unsigned ones are respected and valued.

You're nice, but oh that other teacher

Every teacher has listened to children's complaints about school, classroom rules, or another teacher. Of course, within her own classroom there is no problem; she's free to resolve a complaint in any one of several ways. When it concerns other teachers or administrators, professional etiquette requires her to tread a narrow pathway. Ethically she must not undermine their authority. Humanely, she must remain a real friend to the child. Silently she may agree with the child, but this won't help his plight.

An Action to Take: Be a friend of the court. Have a short, sympathetic talk with the complaining child. Establish your feelings in warm, general terms. Explain that he must iron out his problem with the irksome teacher herself. Suggest he make an appointment with her. To bolster his courage you can walk the child to the teacher's room, but let him go in by himself.

Garner all the grumpy gripes

Keep a gripe box. Slotted. Decorated if you like. Any child who feels that something is amiss in the classroom writes his comments and drops them in the box. Never, never divulge the writer's identity if the slip is signed. Unsigned slips are acceptable. Quite a number of teachers suggested this device.

If I were king

Each pupil writes a letter describing the classroom he likes—general atmosphere, kind and amount of freedom, type of teacher. Ask him to include new ideas and suggestions. Assure and reassure everyone you will keep the authorship of contents confidential. After you have collected and read these letters, have a discussion. The group can think and talk about which ideas will work and why. It's amazing how many of them recognize the need for courtesy and being soft spoken for everyone else, anyway.

Mr. Gallup's latest report

Five or six times a year have the class write letters on their progress. Remind them—new ideas for changes are welcome. Reaffirm—everything in each letter is confidential, so no one needs to plead the Fifth Amendment.

Constructive Protest and Report Cards

Closely related to constructive protest is an understanding that responsible reasoning is needed before one arrives at opinions. Report cards are highlights in a child's life, and they provide an excellent vehicle for teaching him how to arrive at reasoned opinions, or how others arrived at their opinions.

Several additional dividends come from taking in the child's viewpoint on grades. Foremost, it reminds teacher and pupil that grades are a symbol of achievement along a prescribed line, and that their source is in the achievement, not in any person. Of course you know that the child should not regard them as a bleak token of predestination, but most children need help in remembering this. A graphic lesson can do wonders. Secondly, consulting with the child teaches him in vivid terms that the establishment can be reasonable, that speaking up does pay off.

I thought, she thought = we thought

Three days before official report cards come out, have children make informal cards. List important subjects on the board. Tell the children to copy each name, give themselves a grade for each entry, and give reason/reasons why they feel they have earned the grade. They must tell why or it's no credit. These papers are a wonderful guide in making out printed cards.

The perfect triangle

Inform children—Any objections they have to report card grades are open for discussion in a three way conference: teacher-parent-student. At the conference table talk to parents privately for about ten minutes, and then invite Mr. Complainer, Jr., to join you. If it's a borderline decision, why not yield? The child is in the process of learning when to conform and when to object, and this could be a crucially important step in strengthening his courage to speak up and out.

COMMITTEE WORK

Three, helping one another, bear
the burden of six.

—Old Persian Proverb

Seven-league boots were part of the terranaut's gear of yesteryear. And who are terranauts? Let the youngsters discover a good definition for adventurer. Focusing on a natural link between the students and their fantasies and fascinations opens the door to adventurous committee projects. Tossing a multitude of relevant student ideas into a common hopper is almost a must in preparing for good committee work. Ideas generate ideas. Ideas activate other ideas. When the atmosphere is teeming with ideas, enthusiasm and activity come a few steps behind.

Then is the time to set up framework rules for reaching some goals. If committees are good working units, they are nearly always a trifle noisy. If your committees are too circumspect—beware. Usually four of five groups will develop about as they should; the fifth will cause a commotion. If this other extreme develops, here is a suggestion from a particularly outstanding teacher. It might fit your needs.

The fifth committee is a fifth column.

The class is doing fine except for one committee which is a disorganized, disorderly mess. Steps to take: 1) Review goals and rules of the project with them. Be sure everyone understands what is expected of him. Then you circulate in other parts of the room. 2) If garbled noise and activity persist, warn the unruly youngsters. Then leave again. 3) If you must return a third time, ask group to sit quietly with hands folded. Stand next to them as you do this. After a few minutes let them relax. Later on when you have small groups and one unit is troublesome, you'll only need to take step 1, reviewing the rules and goals; and then if trouble persists, ask the children, "Do you want to sit in silence?" You'll find the children will usually monitor each other.

Proving grounds

Sometimes during committee work or play rehearsals you isolate a child who is impeding progress. Shortly, he pleads to re-enter the group and often you don't feel he's ready, yet you're reluctant to say no. Often you can tell him, "It requires less self-control to work alone than in a group. If you can manage to do two rows of your unfinished math assignment quickly, you will have earned your right to again attempt group work because you will have proved your sincerity and self-control."

Where there's bait, there's a hook

Live animals will hook children's interest every time. This is an excellent way to ease into committee work and to teach the necessary rules as a by-product. Directions: Borrow a cage of white mice, lizards or other critters for a few days. On the morning of their arrival announce to the students: "These mice will be here for only a week." (A definite time limitation adds piquancy.) "You are invited to watch before school; but on bell tone—back to your seats." Then let a few stay and inspect, by special permission.

However, explain that they can't just watch while their classmates are working diligently (of course they will be, won't they)! Suggest that the watchers make a pencil list of ten facts they observe about the animals. (They may quietly discuss the mice.)

Rapt interest carries the day; the naughtiest child will do nothing to jeopardize his ringside seat.

Use your heads, save your feet

A good plan is half the battle. Tell students that the staff of #103 is going to sit in the general's tent and plan the battle. Elicit contributions from the entire class (your staff and your army are exactly the same size. I can almost guarantee that the children will not notice this dual function of your troops). Analyze the following points and put the list on the chalk board.

1. Goal of this project	1. ________________
2. Research – approach – method – equipment	2. ________________ ________________ ________________
3. Mechanics of sharing supplies and equipment	3. ________________ ________________
4. Chairman's role – director of traffic, not the driver	4. discuss orally ________________

5. Compose a schedule of leader rotation if project is a long one.

When the above basic form has been established, break the class into committees. As a general rule avoid launching committees during the first weeks of school. Weld your students into a cohesive class first.

Pot pourri of talents

Balanced committees are stimulating, and make the project in its entirety workable. Think of these facets when you make selections: Place in each group 1) a clever child and 2) a slow one, 3) a long attention span child and 4) a short attention span child, 5) a hard worker and 6) a goof off. It helps if children are compatible; if they're not, switch them quickly and quietly.

Form your own form to perform and inform

Method without madness, the madness of paying so much attention to detail that one loses the overall picture and vision of things to come. A good work schedule for committees or lab sessions helps students retain a sense of direction, hone their ambitions and accurately evaluate their accomplishments. The following form was developed by an exceptional home economics teacher. With adaptions, it readily lends itself to other subjects. Obviously, she passes this out ahead of the lesson; and in slower classes the students fill in the forms together.

I. Items or products needed from the counter.

II. Supplies I will use from the kitchen.

III. Utensils or tools I use and return to counter.

IV. Needed utensils or tools already in kitchen.

V. Listing of jobs which we must do in order to accomplish our task:

Teacher announces this to class, "These may be listed and numbered later in the order that you girls feel would be best to follow. Use the back of the sheet so you can have a detail listing and so you will exactly understand."

VI. Time plan:

Class begins __________ Class ends __________Cleanup starts __________ Product complete by __________Judging done __________

VII. The storage arrangment which I have made for this lesson is:

VIII. Evaluation of this laboratory:

A. The best part of this lab is:

B. We still can improve in these things:

Now for a few parting words of wisdom, from several experienced teachers, about initiating special committee projects:

Plan your skeleton program. To sell your package, use intriguing 30-second and 60-second commercials for a week or ten days ahead. Feed in these tidbits innocuously and systematically. And after all this, if you don't have enthusiastic volunteers on launching day, drop the project. Frankly tell the students that it is because of their lack of response. If you do this without any disappointment in your voice, you will have many grateful students. Respect for you will grow immensely because you have respected their preference. In most cases you can present the idea again later on, and the class will embrace it wholeheartedly.

CONCLUSION

Lively, sharp communication in moderated tones adds zip and gusto to learning. Children are not raucous. They merely need guidance in learning to differentiate between their indoor voices and their outdoor voices. When children sit in quivering (or even non-quivering) silence, the fear producing it causes their thinking to stagnate. The first need is to establish reasonable whispering standards and then to teach the youngsters how to modulate their voices, rather than to correct or scold them out of faulty ways.

The next step is better classroom discussions. Oral busy work is not as apparent as written busy work, but it's not much of an improvement. Working to improve one's skill in the art of group discussions can be a scintillating and inspiring experience for any teacher at any age, anywhere. And think of the added hours in the class's learning week. Formal group discussion provides the discipline of having a well defined goal. It is a special method in itself.

Often overlooked, but of vital importance, is the opportunity to actively and constructively teach students how to intelligently protest when their ire is aroused or their sense of justice offended. Teaching constructive protest is a very civilized and humane move. We teach them to respect authority. We teach them to accept authority. We must teach them how to vent antagonistic feelings in ways which are at once profitable and proper.

Finally, I included some brief suggestions and plans on committee and lab work along with the choice morsel of advice: Don't force special projects. I'm confident that if you try any of these ideas they will give your work fresh impulsion.

3 Self-Government--Individual and Group

There can be order without freedom but there can be no freedom without order.

—John Gardner

Chaos is a crimped freedom. In teaching individual and group self-government, we must show children how true law brings freedom in exchange for obedience. True law evokes, not curbs, a higher form of freedom, since relying on a body of sound laws opens the way for more expansive thinking and actions. Traditional folklore repeatedly imparts that school constricts individual rights. Admittedly true today, this was far more often true in the past. It needn't be true now. However, we may dispel these inward, limited expectations of school, this limited definition of order, only by proving differently to our students.

In this chapter we will present some techniques for helping individual students learn more of self-control, and for setting up effective, fair ways of group control. Next, we'll consider making and changing group rules. Trial and error is rarely a tidy process, but the whole feeling engendered by a willingness to try reasonable change encourages a vitality and freedom which promotes greater growth and self-contained stability in the long run.

Elections are a cornerstone to our concepts of democratic processes, but many elections are far from democratic. Real issues remain hidden. Sometimes, too, voters choose inferior candidates over better ones—and many times for inferior and warped reasons. Nonetheless, this is no reason to discard the process of choosing by election. It simply means that the electorate concerned needs guidance and encouragement to think and reason more lucidly and farsightedly.

Today's older students fully understand their right to be heard, but not all of them seem fully aware of their duty to know what they're talking about before they speak out. What an opportunity we have with younger students! What better time will we ever have for reaching their thought than in their school elections? How precious are these moments for teaching them to look beneath surface charms and persuasions, for teaching them to hold their thinking above mass hypnosis, for helping them become aware of subtle influences on their decisions. If we can teach them that the machinery of a well-run election guarantees nothing, but that the thought processes of the voters are all important, we will have done much.

Next in this chapter we'll take up several ways of defining and distributing student leader duties. Patently clear responsibilities promote sensitive, yet well-directed leadership. Although many youngsters show a demonstrated talent for leadership, many more have this natural talent lying dormant, just below the surface. Leadership requires more than a flair for it; the largest elements are good training and the desire for responsibility.

Some good ideas on developing teams within the class are also included in this chapter. Channeling some of the youngsters' spirited energies into worthwhile team goals directs their competitiveness away from classic teacherbaiting challenges.

INDIVIDUAL SELF-CONTROL

A self-disciplined or self-controlled classroom is simply a room full of self-controlled individuals. Each child must learn to govern himself, accurately appraise his own conduct, and understand how important his own conduct is, before he can be a real asset to group self-control.

As I interviewed many outstanding teachers I questioned them about individual student self-control. More and more I realized how each teacher's attitude permeated the classroom. May I offer for your consideration some of their techniques for helping a youngster get a wider, more complete picture of his conduct, or for helping a child who may be stumbling?

Turn with me, please, to the fact that children live in the now. Tomorrow is forever. Yesterday hardly was. Here are several ways of showing them that tomorrow starts with today.

It's a matter of public record

A good citizen chart. Hang a large pocket chart on a wall. Print each child's name on a colored card and insert it in a niche. When a child misbehaves, the teacher asks him to remove his card. IMPORTANT: The student himself must do the removing—not the teacher. He then hands it to her. She dates it on the back and puts it into her desk drawer. On Friday every child whose name card is still on display may get it and paste a star after his name. This social event is a highlight of the week, and is much treasured by the children. Monday brings a fresh start. Preferably, each student whose card is in the desk drawer replaces it himself in the chart. Since the chart is an encouraging and refining technique, it is most effective in a classroom where basic control is an established fact.

Custom tailored for individual fit

Ask your small, unruly crony to stay for an after-school visit. As you talk, work. Rule a check sheet outline on tag or shirt cardboard. Making each copy fresh makes each child feel his uniqueness more than a ditto form would. Ask him for suggestions on improvement points. Start with the points which he feels are most important and on which *he* feels he is most apt to have success. Then, for a week, he's to keep the list at his desk and maintain a record. Over the week-end send the card home for a signature. Keep these charts for about four weeks. Generally speaking, try not to have more than six students doing this at one time. Figure 1 shows a sample form.

More than pillar to post

It's all well and good to speak of self-control—but why should a child develop this? From his viewpoint? Some teachers have found it helpful to have each student sit down, usually in the autumn, and have him decide on *his* goals for *this year.* Just the act alone helps to prune the vague and grandiose and leave a realistic residue.

Success ✓ Chart for Peter Improvement ✓– Failure o	M	T	W	Th	F
Peter tries to: Be ready for work when bell rings	o	o	o	o	
Stay in his seat	o	✓	✓–	✓–	
Not to interrupt others	o	o	o	✓	
Use library time well	o	✓	✓	✓	
Not to run or skip in halls	✓	✓–	✓	o	

Figure 1

Signed and counter-signed

A good class discussion in terms of day-to-day behavior standards is a splendid preliminary to using this record sheet. If you elect to set this up on a weekly basis, it makes a good record for the quarterly grade and saves the youngsters from the need for midnight conversions. Straight A students usually receive some sort of public award.

Name____________________ Room________ Date__________

	Above Average	**Average**	**Below Average**
Self Respect			
Courtesy			
Thoughtfulness			
Dependability			

Student is to score himself on the above points and then sign.

	Above Average	**Average**	**Below Average**
Self Respect			
Courtesy			
Thoughtfulness			
Dependability			

Teacher is to score student and then initial ______________

Important: Teacher and pupils must share a common understanding of what these terms mean, and why the qualities matter.

Silver standard

Three weeks' good behavior is the security behind this award, which can be typed on a primary typewriter (extra large type) and decorated with a silver notary seal and red ribbon.

Date ____________________

CERTIFICATE OF AWARD
(Silver Seal)

____________________ has shown very good conduct for three weeks in Room 21, Oakton School.

____
Mrs. Elizabeth Arras
Fourth Grade Teacher

Also, this teacher divides her room into four or five teams, and uses a plus and minus point system covering many aspects of conduct. A silver certificate earns five extra points for a team. A gold certificate brings 15.

Gold standard

The security behind this award is three silver certificates. The design is the same as above except that the message reads: "____________________ has shown exceptional behavior in the classroom. Your child is a good citizen of Oakton School and Room 21." Naturally, use a gold seal in place of the silver.

TAKE THEM TO THEIR LEADER

A first task for any supervisor–whether he's running a steel plant or leading a Cub Pack–is to let people know what's expected of them. Effectively, he must let them know the priorities and scope of their responsibilities. One unusually courteous teacher distributes the following very complete bulletin to his classes at the beginning of the year.

Sample bulletin

Needed Information
For Mr. Gillies
Mathematics Class

CLASSROOM PROCEDURE

Try to acquire these traits and habits

1. Raise your hand when you have something to say.
2. Be in your proper seat and ready to work when the bell rings.
3. Discard paper and other rubbish only at the beginning and the end of the period–the first and the last five minutes.
4. Get a note if you are tardy. Remember, three unexcused tardinesses constitutes a U–for a citizenship grade.
5. Get permission before leaving your seat or the room. Going to the pencil sharpener is the only exception for leaving your seat. Also remember, you must always sign out before you leave the room–even with permission.
6. Quietly follow the teacher during a fire drill. The boys in the last row should close the windows.

Try to avoid these antics

1. Speaking without being called upon to do so.
2. Chewing gun or eating candy.
3. Writing, marking, scraping on or generally mutilating desks.
4. Writing and passing notes.
5. Talking to your neighbor when you should be working.
6. Being tardy.
7. Being at the pencil sharpener with another person.
8. Talking or horsing around during a fire drill.

EQUIPMENT NECESSARY

1. Unlined paper . . . . regular 8½ x 11½ inch typing paper.
2. Pencils . . . Always sharpened and preferably #2 (no drawing pencils or magic markers, please).
3. A 12 inch ruler. It should also have one edge with millimeters and centimeters on it.
4. Protractor, Compass, Book Cover.

TESTS

1. *Importance* The tests results will constitute the major part of your quarterly grade. *They are extremely important.*
2. *Tests Are Announced* All Tests will be announced in class several days in advance.
3. *Material Covered* Tests will usually cover several parts of a chapter or sometimes even a complete chapter.
4. *Re-Testing* The tests will usually be given only once. Only in unusual circumstances will a test be given a second time.

5. *Absent From Test* Students absent from a test have the self-responsibility of making arrangements to take the test within two weeks.
6. *Number of Tests* Customarily, there is a test given about every two weeks. Therefore, there are from four to five tests in one quarter, a nine week period.
7. *Letter Grades* Numerical grades can be converted to letter grades with the key below:

   A. . . . .95-100 D. . . .70-74
   B. . . . .85-94 F. . . .Below 70
   C. 75-84

HOMEWORK

1. *Day of Homework* There will be an assignment in mathematics on Mondays in the 7th grade and Tuesday and Thursday in the 8th grade.
2. *Length of Homework* During the first semester it should take about 30 minutes and during the second semester about 45-60 minutes.
3. *Day Assignment Due* Homework will be discussed, checked, and collected the day following. These papers will be filed in a folder given to each student.
4. *Grade* There will be a cumulative grade given for homework each quarter. The grade will count as one test grade.
5. *Delinquent Assignments* Failure to do these weekly or bi-weekly assignments will place a student in serious trouble. Only one day is allowed if the student was not absent.
6. *Excuse for Not Doing Assignment* Usually there is no excuse. The only exception is a person who was absent. In this case this person has the self-responsibility to get the assignment and to turn it in within a week.
7. *Heading The Math Homework Paper* Follow the example:

Joe Doe
Dec. 9, 197–
pp. 39 ex. 1–8

Math

DISMISSALS

1. When the bell rings, the class is *never* automatically dismissed. The teacher must verbally dismiss the class.
2. Each day of the week the class will leave room differently. But, any day of the week will be the same during all the weeks.

3. *Monday* The first row will leave first, then it will be followed by the second, third, fourth, and the fifth will be last.
4. *Tuesday* The second row will leave first. Then it will be followed by the third, fourth, fifth, and the first row will be last.
5. *Wednesday* This same procedure will continue with the third row leaving first, etc., through the rest of the week. On Monday this procedure will start over again.

SOME FINAL POSITIVE SUGGESTIONS

1. Participate in classroom discussion daily.
2. Ask questions when you fail to understand a concept.
3. Make an appointment with the teacher for a before or after school session if your misunderstanding persists. Please do this soon or immediately after you have trouble because I will not tolerate a class full of people after school the night before a test.
4. Be punctual when coming to class.
5. Hand in your homework promptly and make sure:
   a. It is neat.
   b. Each problem has been properly numbered and circled.
   c. The paper is correctly headed.
   d. It is checked and recorded.

If you take note of this entire bulletin and follow these suggestions, you will find yourself thoroughly enjoying and learning mathematics this year. Finally, and hopefully, you will be doing well, too.

Ben Gillies

MAKING AND CHANGING GROUP RULES

Probably the most important of all disciplines is that of sharing; it's a major key in all communication. Understanding, empathy, self-discipline,—all these traits are required. Sharing the experience of making and changing group rules deepens and enlarges children's sense of community. Before rules are adopted, it's wise to have a thorough class discussion, which should include questions and comments about suitable sanctions for each rule adopted.

Later on (happy day!) you may find that you have a room rule which is superfluous because no one ever breaks it . . . . or sometimes because the school has issued a new blanket rule, e.g., no toys at school. This opens a fine opportunity for you to lead the class through the process of deleting a rule and substituting a more necessary one. Learning the process of gradual change is in itself excellent training, and an often needed experience for youngsters.

Again, most of the material I collected for this topic was during interviews with outstanding teachers in their rooms. If the classroom itself had a good feel, I included the teacher's suggestions even though some seem a trifle bland.

Fie, fie, fie, Sir John

Or cool it, Johnny, old pal. Group self-government can start very young. Try the student-chairman system to check the amount of whispering and roaming in the room. The term of office is one week, and the plum of privilege is the right to name one's successor.

In the beginning . . . . .

Use the first five or six days of school to establish definite patterns and procedures. The following items are basic guidelines which need to be tailored to fit the class.

1. Children make class rules, five to eight of them.
2. Children select own seats, which are changed five or six times during the year.
3. Children choose workmates, at least to start.
4. Learning is the first goal of the room. Anything which interferes with this will be questioned.
5. *Respect* of others is all-important. Children don't have to like each other, but they must extend respect. And they should know that mature people, of any age, like people–of any age.

You may break up the first week of conduct training, establishing procedures, and general orientation with school work related movies, stories, records, and news discussions, but avoid trying to teach much academic material, especially important units. A properly chosen movie with a good introduction discussion beforehand and a question and answer period afterwards can be both instructive and profitable.

This bill was sponsored by . . . .

Class develops six or eight important rules. The first person who made the suggestions for an adopted rule is named author. When the rule is made, the class establishes a suitable deterrent against breaking it, and a monthly reward for consistently obeying it.

Example:

CLASS RULES

1. No fighting–Johnny Roegge
2. No gum chewing–David Junior Jones
3. Pay attention–Brad Carlin
4. Only soft whispering–Moya Gallagher
5. Study hard–Elizabeth Wood
6. Stay in your seat–Peter Johnson

REWARDS	DETERRENTS
Extra movie	Refrain from class discussion
Candy	Write sentences
Extra recess	Apologize

Talk it over . . . . before it happens

Read library book stories to the class on problems similar to those you want them to consider . . . fighting, shyness, etc. After you finish reading the story aloud, discuss the salient points in the story. When the discussion is on a good tempo, shift emphasis to the problem as it applies to your neighborhood. A book captioned *Winning Friends, Keeping Friends,* part of a series, was written by Mountain and Mason, published by MeCormick-Mathers Press, Kansas City, Mo., is a splendid source of information.

An ounce of prevention

At beginning of a class announce that the student council representative will take a group grade to the office directly after class. This mark will have two sections: one will reflect conduct and the other will reflect the quality of work. If needed, names of trouble makers will be added so the whole class need not suffer as a result of the antics of a few. The swiftness of recognition has a magical touch. Naturally you'll need the co-operation of the office but this method is a pleasant, efficient way of promoting a good atmosphere. It is invaluable for helping a substitute or a new teacher.

Infraction and penalty

Both are known quantities. A rule is only as good as the enforcement of it. Each time your class decides through discussion on a necessary rule, also have them consider and establish a basic fixed penalty for infractions of it.

According to Blackstone

A rule is only as good as the enforcement of it. Each time the class discussion results in a necessary rule, also establish a basic fixed penalty for infractions of it.

Our room is financially independent

Class dues of 5¢ a person per week add up to a workable sum in a short time. These monies can be used for school magazines, assemblies, parties, treats, a reserve pencil pool. Most often, class officers take entire responsibility.

Every kingdom has different laws

Elect officers for a two-week term by secret ballot or show of hands. Since these offices are student-elected, don't remove anyone except for malfeasance of duties. Make a permanent chart with pockets for temporary name-card insertions. Officers and their duties:

Chairman
Waits for order in morning
Initiates pledge
Leads song

Supply Officers 2
Distribute fresh paper
Care for equipment

Librarians 2
Arrange book displays
Maintain order

Custodians 2
Empty pencil sharpener
Draw draperies for films
Switch lights
Clean art project messes

Master of Ceremonies
Leads current events discussions
Handles details of elections

Traffic Officers 2
Lead lines
Hold outside doors

Mailmen 2
Return papers
Deliver out of room messages

Chalkboards 2
Clean boards
Clean erasers
Hand out chalk . . . in some cases

This time, write the rules

Suppose almost all of the class has thoroughly discussed the rules they've created, and most are abiding by them. Still, there are a few youngsters who haven't absorbed the meaning of the situation. Briefly review with them why we have rules and then ask them to copy the rules from six to 12 times.

"12 good men, tried and true"

When an individual repeatedly disrupts the class by breaking the rules the group itself has established–turn the class into a jury and explain they are to discuss suitable punishments for continual infractions. Explain that you, as judge, reserve the right to modify recommended punishments. You might add that you have earned this right on the basis of your wider knowledge of rules in the other rooms in your building.

SELECTING STUDENTS FOR OFFICES

Occasionally one clique wins any and all elections. Sometimes they are "natural" leaders, other times they are the magnetic personalities, social set children, or a smoothly agressive few. Once in office they acquire experience, and a reputation which given them even more self-confidence to reach for the next leadership role.

Several good reasons exist for increasing the number of boys and girls in the act. Leadership is not merely a natural talent, it is also a trained one. The fellow who almost won is usually a little short-suited in one personality facet. He could gain much from a term of office coupled with good guidance from you or from another child who previously held the office. An office is a powerful influence . . . . it can stretch a student into using dormant abilities.

Sociometric plotting is a good device for helping a teacher learn who is the most popular in the group,–to learn the lay of the land–but it would be foolish for any teacher to go overboard by following only what she learns from this. The goddess popularity doesn't distribute her favors on a fair, a democratic, or even a thinking basis. She is also fickle. Sometimes personal popularity is won on superficial qualities, and children get a healthier perspective when they see character qualities which make for long term success at least partly recognized. Respect for children doesn't require teachers to abandon all their influence. Nothing rules out a blend of adult and student opinions, and a lot of precedent rules it in. Most government and industrial leaders use their earned right to influence appointments under their responsibility–not by arbitrary edict, but by friendly persuasion and nods of approval. In the last analysis, the schools are trying to train a generation of active, enlightened citizens, not a generation of charming salesmen and passive customers.

The electorate as well as the elected gain by broadening the base, since the electors often need their ideas expanded on who makes a good office holder, and why.

Weighted Point System For Holding Office

This system helps to regulate the amount of time any one student spends on extra activities, it overcomes in-group constriction, and at the same time it avoids the pitfalls of teacher manipulation. The setting up of a system like this is a natural chore for the Student Council at the junior high school level.

Points are assigned to each elected office according to its importance and its consumption of time. No student may have more than a specified number of points per year. Example: Nine points, and the student must retire with honors. Points are cumulative.

Five-point Offices

Student Council Officer	8th Grade Officer
Girls' Club Officer	7th Grade Officer

Three-point Offices

Student Council Member	6th Grade Officer

Two-point Offices

French Club Officer	Band Officer
Stamp Club Officer	Safety Council Secretary
School Representative to District	Athletic Captain

One-point Offices

Room Officer	Special Drive Chairman

This is a simplified example: the program is even more effective when there are thoughtful gradations within these categories. Another thing–a child may not run for an office which puts him over the legal limit. Thus, he and his friends are encouraged to think and plan ahead: "Now let's see. Our buddy, Charley, is already president of the stamp club. If we sponsor him for a student council member, then we can't use him for 7th grade vice-president. Where would he do the best job? Which job would he prefer?"

Election by show of hands

Elicit nominations and put them on the board. Each child then buries his head in his left arm on his desk. A student stands at the board and calls each nominee's name. Children show their preference by raising their right arms. If they raise their left arms, they spoil their ballot.

Australian ballot

Ditto and cut ballots ahead of time. Have children vote in back corners of the room, but place a judge's table in front center. Choose a judge, a ballot opener and a tally keeper. You'll need to teach younger children how to keep stick tally. Each step of the election is an opportunity for succinct explanation of a similar step in government.

Selection, not election

Occasionally certain youngsters win every election, and this clips the leadership development of other children, some of whom have real potential. To counteract the unthinking tyranny of the clique, put six, eight or ten names in a hat and let a child pick a slip. Thus you control the situation insofar as you know a reliable child will be chosen to represent the room, you broaden the number of candidates beyond the usual winners, and no child knows for sure whether he was in the running.

Duties of Student Leaders

Most jobs for younger students almost define their own limits, e.g., eraser clapper, chairman of broken crayons. The posts older children earn are defined by club rules and school tradition. The only major job which often has an aura of vagueness is that of line leader. I recommend that you sit down and write a point by point duty description. Since this is so individual, I have included only one example given to me during the interviews. I hope it includes the right clues for helping you to write your own job description.

Rod of the empire

Choose a boy and a girl for line leaders. They are actually class leaders for a week. If they do especially well, the term of office may be extended another week.

The leaders walk at the head of the line going to gym or the auditorium, or the playground, or another class, or at dismissal. Leaders halt the line if there is talking. Either they wait for quiet, or they go back and send the talkers to the tail of the line. The teacher walks at the middle or end of the line.

After gym of playtime one leader chooses by rows or individuals those who are ready for drinks. The other leader holds the drinking fountain. At dismissal the leaders check to see if desks are cleared and gym shoes are in hand to take to lockers. They pass flyers and notes to take home.

At indoor playtime leaders take the nominations and conduct voting for a game to play, and they then direct the game. They keep reasonable order.

Leaders choose their successors, not best friends but children likely to do the job well.

TEAMS WITHIN THE CLASS

Ball teams! Swimming teams! Scout teams! Teams are fun! Team grouping brings an evolutionary step into the classroom; it helps students acquire complete self-control. It prepares them for required behavior change, making them aware of the shift towards more self-responsibility. The pivot agent in this method is the student monitor or captain. . . . . . "brethren of a common lot."

So many earnest graduates come out of teachers' college convinced of the importance of respecting the inherent rights of young children. Great tact and love are in their hearts as they plan to establish a truly democratic classroom. And the first thing they know, they have a gang of youngsters and a condition which the Greeks probably had a word for–but the word was not democracy.

Often much of the trouble can be traced back to the children's earlier training which may even have been excellent of its type. If you find yourself teaching in a school where most of the staff are benevolent authoritarians, your students will arrive in your room trained to these methods. This must be the starting point for change. One trains a child to swim in shallow water first.

A team arrangement makes for a transitional level which is almost vital in a reach for more self-responsibility and independence. For example, children who transfer from church-run schools to permissive suburban schools often get into trouble, not because they're mischievous but because handling all the sudden freedom is just too much for them. Democratic method in controlling students is a plant which grows slowly and sturdily through years of training. It doesn't sprout overnight, nor (usually) will it break in high winds.

Almost any one teaching in working-class neighborhoods tells of feeling among the students a resistance to the whole institution of school, a resistance rarely found to the same degree in "professional" neighborhoods. Often blue collar parents place less value on formal education than other parents do; frequently their own school experiences were sorrier, and consequently they send their offspring to school primed with an attitude better suited to SLUSH, the slippery cereal, and its slogan, "It tastes so awful it must be good for you."

Teachers in these neighborhoods may lean to authoritarianism because of large classes, retarded behavior responsibility among the youngsters, and a few other important factors. The snowballing result is a far more competitive feeling between teacher and student for control. It's this exhausting tension, and not the actual teaching, which makes assignment in these areas so difficult. Obviously, the long range solution is to change the students' attitudes, but a short range device which helps some, and doesn't interfere with long range effects, is to get the youngsters in teams competing with each other. Please keep changing teams and team membership on a monthly or six weeks basis.

The most powerful weapon you have to dissolve their antagonism for school is respect, not love. Respect is power. Pointedly showing esteem for their individuality makes real inroads on winning them. Please be very slow to ask for their respect, at least in so many words: your face is already higher on the local totem pole. Respecting you is a duty they've been told about. Your duty to respect them? Perhaps no one has told them much about that. Most of their teachers and parents love them with a love which the French say is "loving from high to low"; genuine respect meets people eye to eye. There's hardly a better contribution you could make to building their self-respect.

The good guys get a party

Monthly, students compete for a best-behavior prize. Divide the room into say four groups of six or seven children in a unit. If your class is larger, have more groups, not larger ones. Students choose group membership, and each unit has a secretary who keeps an accurate record of plus and minus points. Good actions bring one to three points. Negative actions subtract one to three points. The winning team gets a 20-minute party usually held during an art period. They may invite the others, or they may decide to celebrate aloof in royal splendor. The refreshments–a glass of punch or a little candy, no more.

Lingo bingo

This game is included here because of its potential for building team spirit. Inner city children ask for this game again and again–even though, through no fault of their own, team playing is not one of their long suits.

Directions: Explain the rules and choose the first leader.

1. Each person writes a word, any word, on a piece of paper. 2. Leader marks a letter on the board. 3. Each child crosses out in his word this letter as many times as it appears. 4. Leader puts another letter on the board. 5. First player to complete his word calls "Lingo bingo." 6. Leader asks, "What is your word?" 7. Player pronounces his word and spells it slowly. As he spells, the

leader crosses out letters on the board. 8. If word is spelled correctly and all letters are on the board, the winner gets to be leader. If he is short on either point, he remains seated.

If a few students won't join in heartily, don't scold. Let the other children coax them. After the group has learned to play this game as individuals, have them form teams.

CONCLUSION

Just as a person with a musical ear can tinkle away on a piano and learn to play tunes, or use the same talent and learn the laws of chords and harmonies and thus be liberated into a scope of choice between nursery jingles and concertos—so the right concept of justice and law can bring to students and teachers alike much greater freedom in all their affairs.

A sense of law in the hearts and minds of individuals is the only reliable means of self-government, individual or group. Modern law is not found in statute books; it is recorded there.

There's nothing wrong with authority. Tribal law, a primitive, personalized rule over chaos, is by nature normally quite authoritarian. A benevolent authoritarian approach is often the first step in gaining a control in a classroom. So far, no harm done. In spite of all that has been said and written, many teachers sincerely like this approach and they don't mind working for authoritarian supervisors. There's an honest consistency in their philosophy which deserves respect, even if we disagree with it.

The real wrong comes when a teacher decides that she herself responds to and understands democratic processes, yet her class is so low caste that its members are incapable of learning or appreciating the value of self-government; therefore it's a waste of time preparing them. Whatever its cause, this dual concept of native worth reduces her long range effectiveness to the point at which the kindest thing she can do for all concerned is to find a school where she thinks she is among equals.

As we work with youngsters on the subject of individual self-control, we usually start by helping them with their classroom conduct and then extend our concern to helping them take responsibility for supplies, books, homework. Simultaneously with this we also initiate ways for the group to make and enforce its own rules. As the group develops as an entity, leaders emerge. We have discussed various ways of guiding their paths, building their numbers and extending and expanding the group's concept of who makes a good leader and why. The weighted point system for holding office is impersonal yet it can be thoughfully designed by a student council.

It's hardly news to say that teamwork contributes to students' welfare; but several of the benefits are often overlooked. Teamwork and the setting up of various teams is a splendid training step in converting an entirely teacher-run classroom to a setting where children .work far more on self-directed motivation. It's a vital intermediate level. And in those poorer neighborhoods where there's an implicit conflict between teachers and students, setting up teams shifts part of the competitiveness away from the teacher herself and thus frees her to do a more imaginative job of teaching.

4 Care and Maintenance of Property and Supplies

Anytime, anywhere, taking good care of property is an active form of appreciation. It's a sign of maturity and generosity, a grown-up thing to do. The children's heroes and heroines all do it: cowboys spend their lives at it, and so do nurses, housewives, astronauts. Soldiers take enormous care of their weapons and material, including their clothes. It's not a sign of sissiness; it's a sign of manhood, womanhood. It's a technique of life.

In school, perhaps more than in most places, it's also a sign of generosity. The pupils' younger brothers and sisters—or someone else's young brothers and sisters, or new children—will be passing through this school too. Let's keep it nice for them.

The importance of teaching youngsters property care reaches beyond the intrinsic value of the equipment involved to the cultivating of a more appreciative and caring attitude towards the fellow nearby.

Children learn property care by precept, example, and/or experience. It's a normal, natural facet of their training, everyone's training. It's also part of a teacher's training. If the home and community are doing their job properly, teachers do not have much difficulty with vandalism in school. But if the home and the community are falling down on the job, then it's the teacher's privilege to squeeze in this lesson. Care of one's tools and environment is part of the road to success *in almost any definition of "success."*

Mrs. Betty Fitzgerald, first full-time home economist for the New York Housing Authority states (as quoted in the *Christian Science Monitor):* "It is not enough just to give people better housing. You can take a person from the slums, but it is as important to take the slums out of a person's thinking. That will require far more teaching, training, and orientation than anything we've done so far." Mrs. Fitzgerald directs activities for helping Housing homemakers learn better ways and greater resourcefulness in their jobs.

Wanting and knowing how to take care of things is an acquired skill, no an innate talent. Though children seem to have a destructive streak, most lapses are due to ignorance or a careless environment, or to hidden personal problems which no child should have to bear, and which the youngster himself may not recognize. More of this later.

CARE OF SCHOOL PROPERTY

Its good to remember that, when youngsters don't appreciate what is done for them in modern, convenient, efficient, handsome school surroundings, it's because they have no measuring stick with which to compare past and present, then and now, here and there. You'll have a great time showing them the immense changes in school since grandma was a girl. A citizenship meeting is a good setting for this discovery, or this would be a good project during the orientation training while you're emphasizing class room procedures. Example: THEN AND NOW–A lesson towards appreciation.

Prepare the way by discussing with the children the abundance and affluence of American life. Have them mention comforts and luxuries the simplest American family has today which the carriage classes of 100 years ago didn't expect: central heating, running hot and cold water, electric lights and refrigerators, telephones, TV, self-operating elevators, fruits and spices from all over the world–the year around; and your list can be fancier if you're teaching in a middleclass neighborhood. Then ask each child to bring a picture from a magazine of, for example, an old-fashioned school, bus or car, a pot bellied stove, a kerosene lamp, a slate, or a little red school house. Ask for an ancient text book.

A day or two later, when the children have brought these in, distribute ditto sheets of the format illustrated in Figure 2 and also put them on the board. As different children make contributions, ask them also to fill in spaces on the board. Some classes will surprise you with how much they can contribute about the schools of yesteryear, but in other classes you'll have to supply most of the information.

Dramatize things a little with your descriptions of a dunce cap and a hickory stick. In fact you might want to mention that formerly in England, when a child misbehaved, the teacher or master called in the building assistant, the thrasher, who gave the youngster a whipping. The thrasher was paid four pence for each thrashing.

Wind up the lesson. After class has finished the chart, question them on how this change reflects our overall higher standard of living and schooling. Why do your parents give you milk? Orange juice? Greens? Hot dogs? Along the line you'll pick up the summarizing answer that good food helps them grow up strong and healthy in body. Why does the community give us good school movies on Friday? A good gym? Maps? Lab supplies? Again you'll pick up a summarizing answer from some student that the community wants them to grow up smart and able to think—strong and healthy in their minds.

Whereas many youngsters regard removing hats as a school rules nonsense, they tend to accept a clean shoe requirement because their mothers keep reminding them of the same thing. "Wipe your feet . . . . CLEAN," insists one principal. He requires mudless feet before children enter building and even takes one door post himself. His rule is designed to care for school property. The visible dividend is cleaner hall floors.

More important, however, this act helps to change the tone of the children's outlook from outdoors to indoors. They slow up from an active play pace and become quieter naturally, without the staff resorting to lining them up formally. In many neighborhoods this amounts to superfluous regimentation.

DEFACEMENT AND DESTRUCTION

Destructiveness and creativity are opposed forces in the life of mind. To create is to construct, and to construct co-operatively is to lay the foundations of a peaceful community.

—Sylvia Ashton-Warner, *Teacher*

Item	Then	Now	How to Show Our Appreciation
Transportation	On foot street cars, buggies	Bus, bike, Car in bad weather	Lock bike in rack. Thank driver
Bell	Big... loud bell, rang anytime	Buzzer, electrically controlled	Come in when you hear it
Desks	Bolted, one size, sometimes gouged	Moveable. Adjustable, easy-clean, smooth tops, etc.	Don't jump on them. Don't play with bolts, etc.
Writing Tools	Slates, ink pens, quill pens, bottles of ink, blotters	Ball points, long pencils, felt pens	Keep track of them; use covers, etc.
Books	Used for years and years, small print, etc.	Big clear print. attractive pictures, changed often	Use covers. Leave them at school in wet weather, etc.
Lunchroom	In gym behind boiler or empty room	Cafeteria, hot food, etc.	Eat, don't throw food, etc.
Resource Center or Library	Resource Center didn't exist. Library seldom used	movies, slides, strips, etc.	Handle books with care. Help others

Figure 2

Since property defacement indicates the destroyers' lack of a belonging feeling, lack of responsiveness to the neighborhood's welfare, its mood is more serious than the property damage involved—though the cash cost may be substantial. It's a short step from a general destructive attitude to a self-destructive one.

Students venting their feelings against school is a reaction as old as Erasmus, but the destructive student is still missing the mark. He won't affect the school seriously. His actions rarely touch the things which need changing, or even the things he thinks need changing. And the really sad part is the defacement won't even help his frustrations, except on the surface.

Anyone's frustration is within himself. It's not in the situation—regardless of how incredibly difficult it is. The sources of his frustrations may be so obscured that he doesn't know what they are or what the problem is, but his dilemma is never a problem without solution. A solution exists. He may not recognize it, or perhaps he won't accept it; whether he should have to accept it might take a library of books to explore in some cases.

Meanwhile, though, getting back to the avenues open to a frustrated person or student right now, the snarls can be corrected only in his own thinking and actions or reactions provided he is already getting a fair deal. If he is not, that should be corrected. If he is, then others can help him acquire more insights, more compassion, more tolerance; but he himself has to do the changing. He alone must handle *his* frustration and the rage which caused him to strike out. First, he must develop a more expanded, more understanding outlook, and then an attitude of greater responsibility towards himself and others. Understanding a situation is the best means of escaping it.

Sometimes a child's home atmosphere is full of frustrated thinking by every family member. He arrives at school like a water bucket filled to the brim. A cup full of any discord and he overflows . . . . an incident follows. Many times this involves property destruction.

When you talk to him about it, you'll usually encounter defiance. Be quiet. Listen carefully after you get the child talking, and keep him talking. Listen some more. Most often you'll soon find the defiance is a relatively thin layer covering a thick sense of defeat. So then, when it's your turn to talk you may want to make a pencil list in your handwriting of his specific accomplishments and concrete, small victories while you're talking. Let him keep it.

If it comes out that he feels his study efforts have been permanently neutralized by his poor behavior in general, fortify him with sustaining facts to the contrary. Offer to speak to teachers he feels are prejudiced against him because of his lousy record. You may not change the teachers' feeling, but you'll do much to convince the youngster he has an adult friend–one who will go to bat for him. This alone can be the pivotal point.

Damage calls for restitution, He must, of course, make some amends. If school laws and funds permit, hire and pay him for work to cover the amount of damage. If laws don't permit paying him and the school must absorb the loss, have him work a prescribed number of hours anyway. You might ask the student what the going rate for odd jobs is, and make your calculations based on that rate. Especially good is a job assignment where he can assist a cordial teacher daily. This could be washing the seats and desks in her classroom. The casual friendliness can be a strong counteracting influence or preventative. One school principal helps solve these damage incidents by allowing atudents to sweep halls, wash windows, etc.

Occasionally, if the student doesn't make actual financial restitution when the destruction involves lab equipment or books, it can be a natural move to require him to use the broken equipment. But not for long. If his emotional problem is solved, there's no point in reminding him of it forever.

The above comments are more or less a synthesis of suggestions and ideas various teachers and administrators offered when I questioned them. Here are a few others which, I hope, a teacher's imagination may use or build on, should the need arise.

$3 down and $2 a week

If serious damage has occured, arrange a conference with the principal, the student and his parents, and yourself. Even if the child can pay cold cash–say from a savings account–weekly payments from current income are a better arrangement. The lessons of taking responsibility for one's actions, and respect for public property, will be more indelibly fixed in the child's mind if he has a number of friendly payment meetings with you or the principal.

Picking up the pieces

Meet student objections to picking up scraps of paper in advance. Remind them that if each child picks up one piece of paper, it lessens the janitor's work. 700 children in school would make 700 scraps picked up. This (or any relevant large number) impresses them.

Fresh air, sunshine . . . .

If you have no other suitable task for making damage restitution, have the youngster take a waste paper basket and fill it with scraps from the schoolyard.

PERSONAL PROPERTY

The challenge of working to acquire or keep possessions, whether of spirit or property, makes them more precious to the possessor. Great and powerful men often treasure humility, while the obscure man doesn't place much value on it because the world's temptations haven't tried to take it from him. Prominent people most often value privacy in their personal lives above almost anything else. As a rule middle income men respect property because it usually represents planning and successful, hard work. Poor men value respect for their dignity because so many would deny it.

When a child needs better habits in caring for personal.property, let him make an effort in relation to it. Even a search for teacher-hidden gym shoes compels effort. If he ruins something needlessly, let him work out the cost at going rates for junior odd job helpers.

Here are a few suggestions offered by interviewed teachers, which may provide useful guidelines for your own ways of correcting this carelessness.

A treasure hunt . . . . the treasure?

The child's own sneakers. A child leaves his gym shoes out. Warn him. Second time: hide them. He's not allowed to look for them until the others are getting ready for gym. If the gym teacher makes him sit on the sidelines for being late, that will reinforce the lesson.

Snitch those sneakers

The first time the pupil forgets and leaves his gym shoes out, warn him. Second time, put them in a closet and he must ask you for their return. Third time, he must write a note home which you will sign. When he brings it back, countersigned, return his shoes.

Here, let me help you

A child who refuses to pick up his belongings or put some thing in its place may be helped by standing behind him and literally holding his hands firmly around the object. Together, pick it up and steer him while he puts it away. You need to do this only once. Later, just the words, "Here, let me help you," and starting to walk toward him will bring a "No, I can do it myself." Your answer is, "Show me." Primary grades only.

Pencil Sharpening

Each of your students equipped with his very own quill and knife, bottle of India ink and blotting sand . . . . how's that for a little old-fashioned nightmare? Makes a dull or broken pencil point seem like nothing. Still though, one of a child's most important personal tools, and the only one over which he has any decided quality control, is his pencil.

When writing with a keen-edged pencil, haven't you felt the enjoyment that comes from using a well sharpened tool? Moreover, hasn't it strengthened your confidence in the preciseness of what you're about to write? Somehow, it is important to keep an edge on one's tools.

Worldwide, every young student's siren song is any noisy pencil sharpener. Until students desks come equipped with silent sharpeners, children will feel the magnetic pull of the RRRRRRRR at the window sill.

Since it's normal for kids to want to move about, and sitting still is unnatural, try providing several other valid reasons for students to get up from their seats occasionally—getting fresh paper, crayons. Even an honest count-to-twenty look at the hamsters would be better than faked pencil-sharpening expeditions.

Instinctively, the youngsters know this is a good way to test a teacher and her authority. Whatever rules function in your classroom on pencil sharpening, be sure to adhere to them yourself. Don't pull rank. A single standard for teacher and students enhances and impersonalizes the rules. It makes it easier to gain wholehearted co-operation from the class. This goes for rules beyond pencil sharpening.

Grrrrrr goes the pencil sharpener

Often one youngster sets off a chain reaction, and . . . . . Stop everyone. Mention the need for good judgment. Have they used good judgment? You will not let anyone sharpen a pencil for a while. You'll let them know when you think they've learned their lesson. Wait 15 minutes. Tell them you'll try their judgment again. Repeat several times, if necessary. Denial of a privilege and restoration in a short time is a good step in guiding self-control and judgment development.

Who has the sharpest pencil?

Another name for this game is, "How many of us will she let go to the pencil sharpener?" Stop and briefly ask class a few questions. "Why can't you let them play this game? It's fun, isn't it?" The children will come up with some good answers.

Keep your own little coffer of well sharpened pencils, medium-length or short. As you lend, extract a promise of return. Medium and short-length pencils without erasers aren't as much fun to use as long ones with good erasers. The differences encourage the the children to get their own sharpened at the permitted times.

If I break the point myself

Maybe she'll let me go to the pencil sharpener . . . and maybe she won't. In a case like this you might hand the broken pencil to a nearby pupil and let him perform the honors.

Captain grinder

Daily, one child in each row is in charge of keeping all pencils sharpened. He may go to the pencil sharpener anytime. Rotate this choice privilege, seat one on Monday, seat two on Tuesday.

Trying out a teacher on the matter of pencil sharpening is one of the safest ways a child has of testing a teacher's reactions and authority. Our whole democratic system is founded on the constant testing of authority—so love your youngsters' spunkiness even while you nip their little games.

"I Found It"

One of childhood's most delightfully wide-eyed and vacuous explanations is, "I found it." With a vagueness approaching grandeur it's offered as a cover for moments of social embarrassment. As long as adults are permitted to ease the facts in diplomacy's name, surely we should not be surprised when children find their own polite evasions. Once in a while a child uses these words the way an adult would—he actually did find it.

Of course you'll want to attend to the actions which brought on the need to tell this "stretcher." Generally, it's wise just to let the words fade into the background, and concentrate on helping the child learn to speak with greater straightforwardness. First, let him know you hold honesty in such high regard that when anyone levels with you, not only has he your respect, but you always try to lessen the punishment. And then do just that after he tells you the truth. For instance, you might say, "Ordinarily, I would ask a student to write a page long essay for having taken the miniature shrunken head out of Billy's desk, but since you told me the whole story without my pressuring you, I'll have you just tell me the things you would say without having to write it all out."

Do you value the property rights of a child more than his other rights? Of course not. Do you value property rights of one child more than other children's rights? Again, of course not. Then why not always save discussion on a property hassle until it doesn't interfere with the class's interests? This means not letting an oral lesson be interrupted: it means not letting your attention be diverted from your professional duty to individual tutoring and group needs during study periods. A good class atmosphere is more important to every individual member than is an immediate settling of a marble dispute, so don't let the climate be rippled by this small stone of contention.

Some teachers start each September with a blanket rule. Any "found" money with hazy ownership claims goes automatically to the Red Cross. Interviewing highly gifted teachers on many different topics brought to light that most of them treated minor "I found it" items with a courteous but very brief dismissal. Here are some of the suggestions I garnered:

In order of importance

You're busy with a group discussion. A quiet squabble over a small object develops. Place the disputed object on (or, better still, in) your desk. At a free moment or at passing time call the two children up for a brief talk. Among the questions you may want to ask are, "Where did you find it?" and "Why do you think you should keep it?"

Two, one, zero

Two children, one disputed object, and no decision seems adequate. Take school funds or your own, duplicate the item, forget the incident.

Fibbers' memories often just fade away

Keep disputed object at your desk for a day or two. Almost invariably the false claimant will forget it. The real owner will ask about it later.

A tisket, a tasket

Choose a basket with a top handle. All loose crayons, pencils, pens and erasers go into the basket . . . a good reserve supply for special needs.

All roads lead to Rome . . . . .

And all lost items in room 108 go into a pot. Crayons, bottle tops, money, all of them. Money is placed in an envelope, dated, finder named, but total not recorded. At the end of two weeks any unclaimed item reverts to the finder.

TEACHING A NEW DISTRIBUTION METHOD

Expertly handling of these chores can add 15 minutes to an ordinary classroom day and 30 minutes or more to a poorly organized room. Maintaining an even flowing tempo is as important as the time saved, for it's during moments of minor confusion in passing supplies that many classroom incidents erupt. Joey whacking Harry with a book, for example. When all is calm and quiet, Joey knows for sure that he'll be caught; but during moderate confusion he's happy to take his chances. No matter how skillfully and tactfully the dispute is settled, still it has taken a few more minutes of teacher's time and energy and patience.

A serene atmosphere helps the insecure child, and a well taught routine lends its own kind of stability. Just as a kind and bland person can be very comforting at times, so can a benign, predictable atmosphere be very welcome part of the time. Paradoxically, routine for routine's sake has a deadening cast, but routine with a worthwhile purpose in mind can have an energizing effect. Children enjoy a certain amount. It's economical.

Simplicity would dictate distributing supplies according to the order you would like children to tackle different lessons. Rarely, if ever, offer younger children a choice as to the order in which tasks are to be completed. A child's security rests in a sturdy framework, and knowing what is expected of him at a given time helps, not hinders, his growth–providing, of course, your motives are to help him grow rather than to bring him under your control, and your methods of convincing him are closer to gentle persuasion than to sharp commands. As children grow older, give them first limited choice: "You may do your math or your spelling first, whichever you prefer." Then, as they prove capable of handling this, expand into a three-way choice and larger.

A working model

It's easier to teach five children than 25. Then let them show class how it's done. Use this method when you want to establish a new procedure. Although it may seem slow, it adds greatly to efficiency. For tedious detail, a well-taught pattern promotes freedom in the long run, since it releases time for better purposes. Many classes would welcome discovering that a teacher really has their interest at heart when she asks for rather strict conforming on matters which the youngsters regard as trivial.

Example: Select one row. Give directions to a captain. Repeat directions to entire row. Ask class to watch model row. Choose a second row. Give directions to a captain sitting in it. You give directions to entire row. Again, ask class to watch carefully. Does the second row catch on as easily as the first one did? Which row thinks it could do as good a job as the first two rows did, even a little faster? Finally, have the entire class go through the procedure.

When the clock says . . . . . .

Put morning's study agenda on board. Include starting time for each subject. Instruct paper passers to hand out fresh paper at given times without waiting for you to tell them. If the group is working reasonably well, you probably wouldn't insist that youngsters immediately stop one task and start the next. However, if the class is working half-heartedly and you realize the lesson was a little of a flop, it's a good out for everyone if you announce "Let's start the next lesson together."

Name your weapon

Especially with younger children, be explicit about the type of paper to use for a lesson. It's not for prissy conformity. Well-defined paper directions avoid this: A child starts a lesson—glances at his buddy's desk—buddy's using a different paper. First child gets a piece of it, starts again, looks in another direction—a third child is using a third type of paper. First child puzzles, gets up and takes a piece of that paper. Indecision can lead to six or eight false starts. Another reason for asking them to all use the same sort of paper is that it makes everyone's paper equal in case you put a display on a bulletin board.

First in responsibility: first in privilege

Let the first student who settles down in morning pass out the first set of papers.

Le self service

As the French would say. Organize room into centers of supplies. Art supplies in one location, paper and pencils in another, workbooks in a third, etc. This way the children have a purposeful reason for getting out of their seats.

Mischievous minority

Have you three or four rather dedicated discipline problems in your room? At least once a day let each pass out a set of papers or set up a piece of equipment. More problem children than this? Be careful. Well-behaved children lose heart if their boisterous buddies get too many of the good deals.

While passing through the portals

As class returns from library/gym have two students stand at the door and hand out item needed for ensuing lesson. Choose the two students ahead of time and place supplies in readiness for their ease.

One thing at a time, please

Explain first worksheet which is usually involved with the day's lesson. Use a second work sheet which needs little or no explanation. Once children are seated and quietly writing their names on first paper, teacher walks around putting second sheet on floor near their desks, or slipping it inside each desk.

The view is great

Place work folders for completed assignments on window counter. This gives youngsters a good reason for going to the window and gazing out momentarily.

A doing class

Three basic rules developed in an art class are easily adapted to other subjects. Discuss these thoroughly with the class and then the first day you enforce them, be a little lenient.

1. When teacher talks–students stop talking.
2. Set exact number of supplies–if child messes, he's out. No seconds. (Usually this means he has had two opportunities–each side of paper.)
3. Announce clean-up time in advance. Child who ignores signal when it's given loses privilege of participating in the next lesson.

CONCLUSION

Learning care for school property is a first step in helping a youngster develop a community feeling with those outside his immediate circle. His enriched sense of identity is worth far more than the preserved property–important as that is.

He's learning a sense of responsibility for his own acts. In many neighborhoods children and adults feel they are helpless pawns of their environment. Every student resents it when too much is done for him without giving him the opportunity to show his strength of ability. This leaves him feeling indebted and yet having no control. By showing children they do have an ability, a control–however small–over a few material things, we are showing them a glimmer of how it feels to be somewhat independent of circumstances.

To understand why things must be cared for, one first must learn to appreciate their value whether the things are tangible or intangible, one of the easiest ways of learning their worth is to compare life with them and life without them. This is not moralizing, but just showing how the facts read. In this chapter we've included a sample lesson in appreciation.

Of course the causes underlying destruction and defacement of property and supplies are often deeply rooted; but sometimes these incidents occur just because the youngsters need a little excitement in their lives. A perverted sense of adventure may be the only cause. While we never lose sight of the goal of helping a child understand himself and his environment, we also have the task of teaching him responsibility for his own actions. At times this calls for restitution in some form, and most often on the school scene this involves the student in working off the claim.

A most sensible way of teaching a child increased responsibility for his personal belongings is to require effort on his part when he neglects them.

Although handling pencil-sharpening needs during the day may seem irritatingly minor and monotonous, it's major to each child faced with an assignment deadline and one blunt pencil point. His pencil is as important to him as a well-adjusted microphone is to a public speaker. Also, pencil sharpening offers children a safe device for testing a teacher's mood. Smooth passing and gathering of supplies and papers in an easy, anticipated manner increases a sense of natural control vitally necessary for an active learning atmosphere.

As the children are constantly testing us on our authority, so we have the privilege of constantly testing them on their readiness to make more decisions and take more responsibility. Everyone keeps stretching . . . . and growing. In teaching the care and protection of property we are also trying to protect the child's happiness, now and later.

5 Using Student Recognition as an Effective Form of Discipline

Since we are all wise and discerning teachers—well, aren't we?—we're acutely aware of the urgent need to help each student realize his native worth. His identity is distinct, expansive and expanding. Necessarily, school work emphasizes a restricted value standard; and the best of achievement and aptitude tests are limited. None fully measures nonacademic talents and qualities; yet motives and desire, responsibility, persistence, stamina, flexibility and self-confidence are prime ingredients in any life success story.

Once Albert Einstein advised in effect, "Be a man of quality, and success will follow." Quality workmanship is always in demand, whether it be clear, concise comprehensive thinking, master craftmanship, or thoughtful and gracious customer service. Building with quality-minded habits establishes the solid foundation which can support either a low slung or a very tall structure, physical or mental.

GENIUS SOMETIMES WEARS A MASK

Periodically, you're faced with a student who expresses unrealistically high life goals, or so it seems. Please, don't be too sure. Your indulgent smile or damning with faint praise could chill aspirations of a daydreaming mental giant. During these years you may be the only person he can talk with freely.

Don't play God. No matter how much insight you have, counsel him humbly and gently. First, have him examine his motives, honestly. If false pride or surface prestige is his main motive, try to correct him so tactfully that he won't know he's been corrected. Sound goals require a sound basis.

Secondly, help him nourish his dreams quietly. Caution him to keep his affairs in Egypt . . . . especially while his aspirations are nebulous. Several good reasons dictate this move. If he talks a lot, his folks, friends and family, will offer advice–and many won't know what they're talking about. Even those who do know can make mistakes from time to time. Let's remember that an experienced Ellis Island immigration inspector admitted Charles Steinmetz with great misgivings. Thomas Alva Edison's teachers saw little promise in him. And then there was the law school dean who told Earl Warren–later Chief justice–he'd never make it in law. (More than one organization would still agree with that dean, but they would have entirely different reasons.) However, of present import to our aspiring young friend is this: as he moves forward, some of his present companions will choose to linger behind, and his progress may provoke the hostility of their envy. Strange, but true. If they're not aware of his higher goals, they won't be quite so tempted to undercut him when they see his daily successes.

Naturally, you would direct his attention to pertinent information concerning his chosen field.

Finally, and most essential, help your young friend set up realistic, intermediate steps leading to his private moon shot–well-planned levels including several points at which he could stop entirely, or shift goals, and not lose his original investment of time and effort–nor lose face. These ascending steps also stimulate indirect benefits:

a) A gradual change of mental and physical environment-expanded horizons. New opportunities do appear. Many times a youngster discovers an occupation, previously unknown to him, which he never would have learned about had he not embarked on his original venture. The second occupation may be better suited to his inclinations and talents than his first choice.
b) Success in grappling with increasingly difficult problems.
c) Cultivating a daily, consistent, building outlook that yields a success spiral outlook.
d) A tendency to work to his known capacity. Often this in turn uncovers or unfreezes other talents.

Is this rather heady anticipation appropriate to tender years? Studies repeatedly show the advantages which accrue to youngsters with clear-cut goals; when undefined desire is changed into defined desire it gains power in application. Rare is the child who aims too high and seriously goes after that over-lofty goal. If you meet one, look for an aggressive parent pushing. Naturally, open-minded counseling is in order in such an instance. Referring to Mr. Einstein again, it was he who felt each educated individual should have two ways of earning a living, a trade and a profession. Confident competence in one need not conflict with the other.

THE ALMOST MIDDLEBROW

Any class will listen, but average/low average classes warmly welcome a brief explanation of I. Q. tests and all their cousins. A forthright discussion clears the air. Experts agree that I. Q. tests are valid but limited, yet even with their limitations the tests can be useful for a preliminary classification. You may want to explain to your class that these tests are tilted for a verbal student who follows directions carefully. As a professional teacher you're well aware of scores varying as much as 30 points for a student; and you know that the tests often don't provide accurate readings on talents such as the artistic or mechanical or on clever imagination. It most certainly wouldn't be out of line to cite a case or two of radically changed scores or to point up limitations of the tests. It helps to save face for children whose gifts lie in other directions.

One great thing you can do is to help lift the curse of mediocrity. A low average student becomes weary in faithfully holding to duty. Often he goes through school feeling nameless and faceless. As a rule he's well behaved or just docile, so he gets no individual attention on that score—yet he doesn't get the glory of good grades. Document his progress with tangible marks of distinction, and you'll reap affectionate gratitude.

This student responds beautifully to the following small technique: He happens to mention an interesting, obscure fact pertinent to your group's discussion, something you did not know. Pause. Then emphasize his contribution by very plainly announcing, "Class, listen to this, I just learned something from Kennie and I want you to hear it, too. Tell it again, Kennie." Believe me, Kennie will glow.

As classmates witness constant recognition of a not-so-clever Tommy's step-by-step gains, the lesson will put life into flaccid hopes and loosen fetters of gnawing futility-feelings the average student gets about his chances of ever being outstanding. School becomes more acceptable because it is more accepting. Top-notch school or athletic achievement and individual worth are not interchangeable terms.

Now, and in the future, every child is capable of expressing the genius of liberty, his heritage of freedom to obey his enlightened conscience within the restraints of law-abiding reason. Incidentally, mentioning law-abiding reason leads us to the subject of teacher reasoning. Nary a teacher owns a bag full of A's, B's, C's, hers to distribute as she fancies. We often speak of giving grades, and yet we well know that student's grades have their real source in his learning participation, not in the teacher's judgment. Thus a more precise thinking suggests a term such as "recorded," "acknowledged," or "issued" grades. Reaching for a more delicate handling of all student efforts, we promote our grading skill in its healthiest perspective and clearest light. (Also see student report card protest, chapter three.)

RECOGNITIONS AND RIBBONS OF THE CLASSROOM

Well-seasoned traditional prizes which fit classroom tenor and tempo may include new accents:

1. Tasks performed for the teacher–Switch them around. Give your most difficult tasks to average students and help them learn to think on their feet. Then use slow students for average tasks. Yes, this leaves bright students with dull tasks–but they like school anyway.
2. Honor roll–Print lists for the behavior and grade elite, as always. Add another list: Up and Coming Crowd. Here include children who have made the greatest improvement.
3. Responsibility in Room–Well-performed duties are acclaimed by letting child name his successor to office.
4. Citizenship Recognition–Teams and a point system are one approach. In chapter three you'll find award forms.
5. Student Tutor–Instead of concentrating on the brilliant student, try an average student. Ask him to help another as soon as he finishes his lesson. See if it doesn't quicken his pace of study.

Here is a collection of refreshingly different ways to recognize hard work and effort which some remarkable teachers have commended.

I Did My Best Today Button

Make a large supply of stringed tags or buttons which read I DID MY BEST TODAY. Distribute these during the last ten minutes of school. At first, be generous. Give one to almost everyone. After a few days raise your standards gradually. By this time the child will be questioned when he comes home without a tag.

Everyone has a best

Surprise younsters one day with a thought-provoking display. Take a set of creative writing papers, and on each child's story underline your favorite sentence or idea. Make no other comment or mark. Mount papers on a bulletin board, one for each child in the class. Then, sit back and watch the joy come into the children's faces when they realize what has happened.

At the end of a well spent day

Rainy, steamy days sometimes make it hard to concentrate on the task at hand. You might announce to the class, "Those who feel proud of their work today–you who think you've done your best in spite of the weather–may get your coats first this afternoon." Sometimes an imp will try to sneak out, too, and generally the class will boo him back into his seat. Occasionally you'll have a child who is overly severe in judging himself, and you'll want to intercede.

Ben Jonson's ghost approves

How many words can you make from the chemistry term, ketoenol tautomerism? What does it mean?–of no real importance, my friend. It's real value is in its 19 assorted letters from which to make lots of new words. Try setting up this contest among individuals or on a girls-against-the-boys basis. Kids really get fired up. A sharp pencil is more important than a sharp mind, and diligence leads over genius in bringing home the laurel wreath.

"A" for "Art," "B" for "Bulletin Board"

Everybody knows you can do a nice bulletin board. Everybody knows you're busy. Everybody does not know that youngsters from the fourth grade up can do some even striking boards. One approach: Choose a theme for a bulletin board. Ask class to think about designs and captions. Suggest they search magazines and talk it over at home with their kin. Each student with an idea makes a simple pencil sketch. You may alter or refine . . . . students never seem to mind. Choose a winner.

Execution: Winner may select one or two classmates as co-workers. In advance remind the winner that you must ratify his choice; therefore he should select co-workers who will help him attain his goal. Usually it's wise for you to be doing desk work while they are cutting and mounting; beyond that, plan to stay out of it. Naturally, you could add a word of wisdom if they're in a tight spot. Please do try your class several times before you decide they're not up to this one; because, by the third time you'll probably be thrilled. This project markedly leavens a group pride in "our room."

Tempting as it may be to exhibit only the best work when it's your room's turn to fill the lobby display case, remember that way is terribly traditional. Your teachmanship and not your showmanship got you your job originally. Now, if you show only the best student work, you'll be letting showmanship and a touch of personal vanity rule your decision. Surely by listening to your heart and tapping your professional skill you'll find a more inclusive standard for deciding. A cross section?—greatest effort?—or behavior problems who have made the greatest improvement?

RECOGNITIONS FOR SLOW STUDENTS

Praise them. Praise them. Praise them. How many times have you heard it? Yet how, exactly, is the best way to praise? When? What is best to single out for praise?

Praising a child in glowing, sweeping remarks ("Sally Lou, you're an angel, an unmatchable jewel,") may scare Sally Lou. She knows she does not deserve top billing, and she's afraid of it; thus, usually she'll intentionally try to blow it. Reduce the scope to

"Sally Lou, you were an angel for giving up your Easter basket for the sick child," and you'll make Sally Lou happy and comfortable. This second bouquet calls for no further action or proof. So obviously the first pointer is: *Be specific* and then leave no dragging strings on which Sally Lou is afraid she might trip.

What to praise? Naturally, there'll be times when a comment like "Sally Lou, that's a mighty pretty dress you're wearing" will be just the thing. Many times, though, it's better to praise an act rather than flatter an appearance. Compliment the child on her actions—especially when she has shown worthy motives—without moralizing. Earmark actions which strengthen her individuality, such as telling the truth, independent thinking, kindness to an equal. These may mean more than her classroom helpfulness, which perhaps stems from docile conformity or servility. Focusing attention on Sally's worthy motive and/or spirited actions means focusing on something over which Sally Lou has conscious control, and she knows it.

When to praise? Who doesn't like to have his virtues discovered and exposed in front of his most cherished friends?

Almost needless to say, there are several indirect ways in which a teacher can praise—e.g. by showing actions such as placing trust, by accepting a child's actions or suggestions as having great merit, even by taking his advice. The following additional suggestions were offered by expert teachers who have had exceptional rapport and success with slow students.

Quiz maker—not a quiz taker

Low-average students get a particular thrill from having their questions used in a quiz. Announce a quiz two days away; everyone who composes a good quiz with correct answers will automatically get a grade check and need not take the classroom test. His questions go into a fund from which you draw in making up your quiz. Often, while class is taking the test, you'll hear a youngster quietly squeal, "Ooooooh, that's my question she used!"

As you introduce this type of quiz arrangement you'll have a few students ask you, "What's the hidden deal, the catch?" Then you'll explain that the purpose of any quiz is to get students to study, and if they pore over the material carefully enough to compose good questions they will have reviewed the material well enough to suit you.

One more r–reliability

She is accurate and responsible . . . let her know it. Having her record grades in your 1st and 2nd grade book informs the class of her standing. If you plan to rotate this privilege, inform the student before she starts her assignment, so there'll be no question in her mind later.

Rank hath power and privilege

Usually upperclassmen enjoy listening to first graders read orally, on a one-to-one basis. Of course, make arrangements through channels, the office, but start your program on a schedule of one 20-minute period per week. Expand it as you deem prudent. Little ones are thrilled with praise from anyone as discerning as an upperclassman. Older children, particularly slow students, feel rewarded and much stronger for the experience.

Mi amigo simpatico

Occasionally, the best person in a room to help a poor reader is another poor reader. Although poor students tend to have low frustration points, many of them relish a feeling of being among equals.

One swipe of the eraser . . . and it's gone

Choose as captain the youngster who made the biggest improvement of the week in your current promotion campaign, be it spelling, neatness, or not butting in line or staying out of trouble. Send him to the board. On the board you have already written this week's spelling words. He erases a word, and then the class must write it. After the class has learned the game, he may erase words in any order he chooses.

By jove, I think she's got it

When an ordinary student comes up with a pearl of a remark, often by chance, pause. Then say, (for example), "Ah, you've caught a moment of truth." Repeat the student's comment for the whole class to appreciate and absorb. If you're more than a bit of an actor on this one, it goes over particularly well.

"Listen my son and you shall hear . . . "

If you have a chart where youngsters are given credit for library books, include the non-reader, too. Give him the same amount of credit for a book if he listens attentively to another student read it aloud.

The newly-arrived like the classic symbols

Gold stars may be old-fashioned and old hat to you, but they put sparkle into the eyes of low-level math students. Give them stars for 100 percent papers. Poorer students haven't received many palm leaves in their school years, consequently they cherish the classic symbols. It's best not to use stars every day.

Once English looked like Greek

Slow readers can show you every word on a page they don't know, but often they forget how far they have come. If a youngster seem discouraged, show him a book written in a foreign language and ask him to read it to you. Of course, he won't be able to read a word. Then show him his current text—and have him count all the words he knows on one page. Remind him that, just a year or two ago, the book in English looked as formidable as the foreign book does now.

Let's look at grades through his periscope

Though a child may have fallen short of your expectations, still from his viewpoint he has gained in knowledge. Try grading on a plus system rather than a minus. Mark the correct answers and then give him a +8 at the top of the page for eight correct answers. A variation: Many math teachers grade papers on a 24/36 system: the 24 stands for the number of correct problems and the 36 the total number of problems assigned. This is not only a very kind way, it is also more precise in the picture it gives the student.

The power behind the throne

For each subject quietly choose teams each consisting of one reliable student and one teetering student. Ask every team to plan a one-day lesson for tomorrow. If you undertake this well into the year, you'll find students unconsciously pattern your style. Low-average students greatly appreciate this honor, and they have an amazing sense of appropriateness. Often it's wiser not to make a general announcement to class on who planned the work; word spreads, and news from the underground is more interesting, nearly always.

One minute of glory

If the public address system in your assembly is available, ask permission to let a reading class use it. Individuals enjoy microphone experience—tremendously. Slow students probably never will have another occasion like this.

Directions: Announce this event ahead of time. Ask children to choose one-minute readings. Interest will zoom. Students will wish, and will need, to weigh stories and jingles as never before. When they want to practice and time their selections, and they will, let them use a tape recorder.

Copyright applied for

Lower echelon English students are tickled when they see their prose and poetry in booklet form. Naturally you'll need a cover with a picture on it, preferably student-drawn. Then include a table of contents with title of each article, author's name and page. Finally put each entry on a separate page, heading each page with the title and the author's name. Use six or eight stories typed, dittoed. Each time use a different group of authors.

Spider tracks across the page

Anything in print looks better, and many slow students despair of their own gawky handwriting. Treat them to the pleasure of seeing their creative writing efforts neatly typed and mounted on a bulletin board. It'll warm the cockles of your heart to see their reactions.

Everyone who works gets paid

At all times display at least one work product for each class member. The traditional method of showing the best only does not reach those who most need the stimulation of recognition for effort. Since good students become accustomed to having their work made public, it's no real thrill to them if one more piece goes up. And less studious youngsters find that their work is never displayed; slowly, through the years they lose amibition; the goal of having their work displayed seems unattainable. Often they believe they'll never get A's or B's either, so why should they work "a little harder" or "keep trying"?

After mediocre work has been posted, you may ask a child to redo it. Generally, he'll accept the opportunity eagerly. Please don't be afraid that this display process will bring down class standards; IT WON'T. It will bring up morale and create more of an "our room" spirit.

Double set of books

Daily, record students' successes in making a genuine effort. Maintain a separate marking book for the purpose. One day, grade each child on his correct paper heading. Second day, give each a grade on penmanship. Third day, give each student a grade on general neatness. Fourth day, a mark on preparedness, text, paper, pen, notebook. Many other facets of school work can be programmed like this. Your students can fully appreciate that these marks will never reach the central office, and still be very enthusiastic about them. From ghetto schools to those in fancy neighborhoods, lagging students everywhere enjoy this system.

Another tour of duty

If any child is repeating a grade, assign a veteran status to him. Explain the role and importance of veterans in the armed forces: they know the ropes the best. Ask your veteran to help the rookies learn the room rules.

CONCLUSION

Recognize means to know again or to show appreciation. As you acclaim a student's worth as an individual, you're doing much for yourself as well. Your awareness of his efforts and motives—the richness of your sincerity and insight in publicizing his strengths—add to your stature, too.

When a child expresses aspirations which reach for the stars . . . . don't cut him down. Pragmatic adult views might not truly fit. Instead, guide him in an intelligent discussion. Tactfully weave into your talk those values and habits particularly needed for his selected role, and stress that he should start working on those today. Striving for quality or excellence of workmanship is one universally-needed endeavor.

Warn the high-aiming aspirant against indiscriminate chattering about future goals. And most of all, help him plan a multi-step blueprint of the future, and advise him to concentrate his efforts on the first step. Intermediate steps will hold value beyond themselves, for they develop confidence and expanded horizons. Often they unfreeze other talents.

A pyramid with a few stars at the top is the old-fashioned idea of a good classroom. It engenders mediocrity, because it emphasizes the concept of limited good, the belief that only a small proportion of students can really make their mark. Its dulling influence lingers today. A more modern concept is one of a high plateau where all along the line students can achieve highly on one strength or another. Honor rolls and other traditional recognitions can be made more enjoyable and effective by adding a tactful upgrading or topical touch.

THREE RULES OF INDIVIDUALITY

Many a modern teacher has ingenious ways of showing students that they are cherished for their individuality. Some basics glimmer through:

1) Each child needs, and can earn, respect for constructive qualities and attitudes which he can contribute to the class scene. Joy, consideration, reliability, responsiveness, sharing or cooperation are essential to any outstanding classroom; but it doesn't take academic aptitude to express these. A slow student can *excel* in one or more of these. Usually he will work very hard to express a particular trait if the teacher directs his attention to his innate ability to fill the role and the class's need for a model.

2) Each child has a continually rising best. He's more impressed with *his* best being displayed than he is with the work of a chosen elite.

3) Nothing activates a child's self-respect more than his knowledge—and a teacher's recognition—that he has accomplished a solid day's progress in schoolwork and the art of self-discipline. Such knowledge and recognition lead to the greatest asset of all, his conscious realiziation of his own worth, his own broadening and deepening identity.

6 Developing Teacher Consistency in Classroom Control

Dominie is a Scottish word for pedagogue. Aye, it's a canny one, too, for it skirts dominion and domineer. A domineering teacher thinks from a personal sense of her own authority, her own ability and her own accomplishments; but a teacher with true dominion (call it understanding self-confidence if you prefer) draws a strength from the inner poise of knowing her own unique identity, and from wise aspirations, humility, and gratitude. Paradoxical as it may seem, the sounder her sense of dominion, the less tempted she is to domineer. Surely, children feel the difference before the first word is spoken.

Though visions of cherubims and celestial trumpets—all on our side—may tumble through our heads, let's remember that the actual post is called school teacher. School is the main field of our work with the young, and in helping children outside of school, we are wise to take on only those tasks which are properly ours. Then we will probably do them well. Even if parents are merely muddling through as parents, still, in the last analysis, rearing the children is their job. Certainly humility's first requirement is that we must not take ourselves too seriously. Earnestly, ever so earnestly, we may believe we are pointing a road to salvation through education, but our words and actions are not that salvation itself. It is fortunate that children are marvelously esilient, and have spontaneously shed—and will continue to shed—many of the consequences due to our mistakes.

Speaking of resilience recalls the frontier stage coach driver's advice to his passengers. As he was strapping mail pouches, traveling trunks and valises to the roof, he cautioned, "Trip's a rough one. Trail is dusty and rutted, there's no springs, the wheels wobble and creak, and the seats are solid wood. Only way you'll ever make it is to ride loose." And this same "riding loose" will get you through many a rough day of teaching.

Along with staying relaxed and calm, gratitude is a most helpful trait in nurturing mental poise. Let's try counting some assets. Compare equipment and books of today with those of 50, 20 or even ten years ago; and rare is the school system which distributes them in incomplete sets. And then salary. It may have taken three skirmishes and a teachers' council posse to the board, but salary results have appeared.

Again, most administrators and principals make genuine efforts to be considerate and fair. They appreciate tone and atmosphere, and certainly they have been trained to realize the vital importance of both. Finally, consider your own training: the formal in universities, the informal in your own childhood, watching for years the style of your own teachers who had ability. Since you have a lot going for you, you should be able to summon the courage and strength to always speak softly.

"What you are speaks so loudly, I can't hear what you say," said Emerson. A balanced life adds resonance to this tone. Personality completeness requires a genuine sense of adventure as well as a philosophy of life, recreations as well as work-derived security. Please don't weasel out from involved living by taking refuge behind committee reports and stacks of ungraded papers—and then call it devotion to duty. If you do hide, please call it what it is—an escape.

Teaching Caps Come In Many Styles

Are you a rumpled hermit? A Mata Hari? A Brooks Brothers buff? Your dress, your personality, add to your distinctive style as an individual. Use the same inherent taste and develop your most appropriate style of teaching—ways which bring out you best, make you come alive. Certainly you have a flair for special subjects and types of lessons. Spotlight those—but the rest of your stage needn't be shrouded in neglect. Your conduct control techniques should blend naturally with the setting.

Nonetheless, you don't need to be a "character" to put character in your teaching. Nor should one be discouraged by reports or experiences concerning misfit teachers some of whom would be misfits in a roomful of misfits. It's the old adage again—don't keep measuring a crooked stick; just find a straight stick.

One teacher claims he's not a kindly shepherd who patiently leads his reluctant flock over the countryside of learning. He claims he's closest to a sheep dog, and he plans to bite at the heels of his little lambs when they frolic too long. He adds, sheep dogs are alert and affable; they bite only to keep their charges out of danger.

While thinking about your own teaching style, mentally picture and feel the classroom atmosphere you hope to have. Carefully cache your dewy-eyed, diffused pictures of your students cheerfully, even eagerly, tackling all your new challenges, pleading for more, and yourself sitting on the queen's throne—in an inconspicuous corner, of course. The millenium is coming, so that dream will have its day; but in the meantime you have another decision to make. Do you want your classroom to be a place where respect is tinged with kindliness, or a place where kindliness is tinged with respect? Balance is the word and balance is the goal.

CLEARING YOUR THOUGHT COMES FIRST

Many of today's teachers try to separate, in their thinking, the child's naughtiness from the child. Often they ask themselves, why did he pull this last one?—do all the kids around him do the same thing?—is it a learned pattern or a fleeting indiscretion? Before discipline is attempted, several more questions need answering. What is the teacher's motive in wanting to cope with the child's latest gaffe? Is it to teach a lesson? What kind of lesson?—that antisocial behavior doesn't pay off? Does the teacher want to get even with the child for interrupting her?—for sidetracking the class's attention?

Every behavior incident involves emotions. Please allow students a few moments to calm down. It would be wise for you to spend this time in trying to thoroughly understand your own emotions. Before you speak or act—clear your thought. Ask yourself:

1. *"Why* do I want this child to obey? *Really?* No other reason?" The more sincere you can be, the more you can level with yourself, the wiser will be your resulting actions and words.

2. "What do I expect of him, *exactly*?" Mentally spell it out. "Would I have expected this of him yesterday? Will I expect this of him tomorrow?"

Deciding wisely what is best for the individual within the context of the group is a master key to classroom harmony. In many cases individual right versus group rights is an imaginary dilemma. The two sides are not necessarily at loggerheads, since every child must learn how to live in organized society. If he doesn't learn it from those who love him, or from those who are concerned about his welfare, he'll have to learn it from those who are indifferent, sometimes brutally indifferent.

Another perplexing question which sometimes mushrooms into a needless mental battle is "the immediate versus the long-term welfare" of the child. It's not necessarily an either-or proposition. Always consider that is can be a three-forked decision point, the third answer taking in both now and later.

Common humanity should prevent us from ever labeling a child as hopeless. Honesty will bring times when we must admit failure in handling a child, and sometimes total failure. We need merely to accept the fact that a teacher and a child have failed in a personal relationship. As the French say, "C'est la vie," or, as the youngsters say, "that's the way the cookie crumbles." But eternal damnation is not a 20th century doctrine. And such failures need not be forever.

If you have an "impossible" child in your class, one whom you don't handle well and in your heart you can't like, try working a trade with another teacher. Take one of her "impossible" cases. You may want to explain to your students that you're trading like teams trade ball players, and you sincerely hope that each child will be happier, and perform better, under the next coach.

DOING SOMETHING ABOUT CONTROL CONSISTENCY

Most teachers are beautifully aware of how much a child can improve in his analysis and attack skills in reading during a year. He does it by working on the task intelligently, day by day, notch by notch. In the same way, you may want to systematically polish your own skills in classroom control, to strengthen weaknesses. Analyze your performance. Too much fluctuation? Is it from day to day, or from child to child? Or both? Focus your attention on just one of these aspects at a time.

Let's say you choose to narrow the distance between individuals, to treat everyone more equally. *Next,* list several problems bugging you: 1) Incomplete supplies; 2) Out of seats without reason; 3) General dawdling in class; 4) Loud talking prevalent. *Third,* concentrate on inproving your skill piecemeal, untangling one knot at a time; attend to the other problems as you have been doing but on the focal problem try various techniques and approaches. *Fourth,* remember the rule of three and five in learning. Alertly drill yourself on overcoming a focal problem for three, four, or five days, depending on your needs. Finally, take up the next item on your list and employ a similar three-to-five day self-drill. (Or auto-reinforcement, if that sounds more modern than self-drill!)

Another avenue to your program of self-improvement is to have the children write a letter or compose two lists. Let them name three things they like and three things they don't like in the room. Lists may be signed or unsigned. These lists may yield many facts you need to know about your control methods, without openly getting into personality discussion.

TEACHING SELF-CONTROL COMES WITH THE TERRITORY

You'll reduce much of your tension and resentment over discipline if you learn to expect to teach some form of self-control as long as you plan to teach children. If your class arrives well-behaved, you can enjoy the luxury of helping them acquire refinements and more tact; but plan to spend the time. Obviously, with less fortunate children, you have to adjust to teaching more basic aspects of behavior. Expecting to spend a block of time and energy on this facet, with every class you have, puts it in its normal perspective; to accept conduct-training as a normal part of teaching helps you overcome the feeling of imposition—that conduct-training is an unnatural extra chore improperly foisted on you by a small number of rascals.

Multitudes of upper and middle class children have responded very well to the following explanation: in all groups there must be control. It can be imposed by others—outside control. This type of control comes from other members of the group or an authority. Or an individual can impose control on himself–inside control. Tell them the choice is entirely theirs, the control can be personal, or by the authority of a teacher or a group. But control there will be. You'll respect any decision they make as long as they live up to it. Incidently, there are many, many inner city classrooms where the children are ready for the responsibility of making this decision for themselves.

Pointedly showing students marked respect impresses children. One way: ask their permission to speak. The request is even more effective in a quiet voice. Limit this type of requesting to a particular period or activity; for example, when a student leader chairs the current events discussion. Avoid the danger of trying it too often or for too long a span of time, since it then degenerates into a phony.

Over and over again with different teachers I asked questions about establishing a good learning atmosphere, routine procedure and conduct training. Each one of them emphasized the wisdom of stressing expected conduct standards and procedures for the first several weeks of school. Voluntarily, and without exception, they added that time spent in establishing basic control will be rewarded many times over. The students will learn far more in the long run, and they'll be far happier.

Then I would phrase the question, "But wouldn't it be wiser to get into interesting projects first, and then work the control bit in, tactfully or subtly?" The answer was No. None of them were willing to change their priority rating. May I add these teachers are *not* old curmudgeons? they are *not* rigid personalities; they are well-rounded, excellent teachers.

Their guideline estimates on the length of time needed to train children varied a good bit, from two to four to six weeks, depending on the neighborhood. One 7th grade teacher in a good suburban school told me that she spends the best part of a 40 minute period every day for two weeks on self-government, room procedures, and customs of the school. This training included a tour of the building–even though the children knew the building, they liked this–and she also had them learn the names, first and last, of every member of the class, and a rather large number of names of children in other rooms. This last she does with a bingo-type card. The only school work she attempts is group discussions focusing on news items which the youngsters bring from home.

"Consistency, Thou Art a Jewel"

It's difficult to be thoroughly consistent in handling misdemeanors. If a teacher is in high spirits, or if the child involved is a good student, teacher is all too inclined to be very lenient. The reverse is true, too. However, the child sees an immediate act, not an overall attitude, achievement level or set of circumstances: i.e., throwing an eraser is throwing an eraser in his book. All those concerned, teachers and youngsters alike, need a guideline beyond personality. Firm rules enforced by an adult with a flexible attitude give youngsters a feeling of security. They know what is expected of them and what to expect. Your flexibility shows up in your one-to-one talk, your firmness and fairness in the action you take.

Generally speaking, general rules about general conditions are a nuisance. Here's an exception. When you must punish a child, relate the deterrent directly to the misdeameanor. Your understanding comments or reprimand will have greater impact if your actions seem penetratingly clear and logical to the child. Examples: In a case of too much talking–make your reprimand polite but brief, and then isolate the child for a short period so he can't annoy others with his talking. Imposing on others' time–impose on his free time. Incomplete supplies–have him count some of your room art supplies, after school, to be sure you have enough for a upcoming project.

List of Drastics

Sometime while you're nestling in your lair, analyze your school world as it pertains to classroom control. One time-honored way: make two lists. The first records, in ascending order, remedial steps which are open to you. The second is a list of annoyances common in your school or classroom. After completing both lists you can slot an offense under the bracket best for your situation. For instance, in some suburban classes children getting out of their seats is no real problem, and any teacher can well afford to ignore it or treat it lightly. In some city classrooms the out-of-seat problem is so acute that a teacher must be firm or she will have chaos.

Example:

Remedial or Correction

Ignore action	Phone home
Stand near child	Dismiss from class
Speak to child	Send for parents
Change his seat	See social worker
Scold child	Student Council
Assign simple punishment	Principal
Keep him after school	Probation
Deprive him of after school privilege	Suspension
Send note home	Expulsion

Misdemeanors

Gum chewing	Tardiness from recess
Eating	"Forgetting" homework
Loud talking	Running in halls
Insolence	Horseplay in assembly
Sharpening pencil	Making foolish noises
Etc.	Etc.

Teacher Reaction

	1st time	2nd time	3rd time
Gum chewing			
Eating			
Loud talking			
Running in hall			

First of all, just making this list will help you clarify your feelings, intentions and actions. Naturally, any teacher who has good judgment is going to use common sense in applying the findings of her own feelings—making exceptions to a rule when circumstances call for it.

The interviews with the many top notch people brought forth splendid suggestions of practical ways of working on this problem of teacher consistency in conduct control:

Fussin' and frettin'

You've had a major upset in your life, or a severe disappointment. Or you don't feel good physically. Tell children you're out of sorts today, and that you might snap at them when you ordinarily wouldn't. It can make you seem more human in their eyes, and they'll let up on their antics because they've been taught at home to be considerate when someone doesn't feel well.

Did you ever hear a noisy teacher?

The kids call it yelling. Make a check list on a slip of paper. Include trouble areas. For example: Raised voice. Sharp tone. Sarcasm. Scolding. Negative expectancy. As you go through a day, check every time you slip.

Don't be a self-appointed judge

Avoid expressing disapproval on a "right" and "wrong" basis. Instead try to express impersonal dislike for offensive ideas. Sometimes a comment, "Such a subject for a 13-year-old to be worried about!" said in a tone of amusement at something quaint can be very effective. Refuse to be shocked, no matter what turn the conversation takes.

Heap big happy tribe

Your class is like a big Indian tribe. Let children choose whether they want to be braves, squaws, or papooses; but there's going to be only one chieftain–you. This appeals greatly to younger children. Incisive wit from the 3rd grade hot line: "You Indians had better be careful; I'm in a mood to start scalping." With that line, teacher, you'll bring down the house.

Garbage in . . . . garbage out

Programmers who work on computers have their own slang. One of their favorite sayings is "garbage in . . . garbage out," which means if they put poor materials into the computers, they get poor results. Sometimes when you have students who are impossible to please, who are bored with anything and everything you have to offer, you might mention how this phrase of the computer world has many counterparts in business and school.

Once a teacher almost flunked

Evaluate yourself every time you issue report cards. Make a list of points: 1) Clear goals. 2) Explicit directions which are brief. 3) Your supplies ready. 4) Positive comments to students. 5) Calm attitude. 6) Controlled voice. Add others which seem important in your case. Tape a few hours of your teaching. Listen to it. Each time you're heard on the tape, grade yourself. If listening to yourself for several hours seems like a big chore, beware! It may mean you really *need* to listen to yourself.

Spout your wisdom freely

You or the class freezes when the principal walks into your room? Leave the door open so he may overhear your teaching, or the industrious, controlled buzz of worthwhile activity, while you aren't aware he's listening. He must evaluate your work–it's part of his job. He'll be glad to hear you at your best.

"Hearken . . . to the soft and pleasant"

Place a tape recorder with a trusted student. Ask him to turn it on for periods of ten or 15 minutes several times during the day. Neither you nor the class is to know when it's on. Later listen for every token of courtesy you extended. Is your voice "the mirror of the soul" you'd like the world to know? Or, in more pedestrian terms, would you want your principal to speak to you in the same tones?

Your best friends will tell you

Ask a good friend to drop into your class during her free period and take notes on your teaching. A fellow teacher can help you clear up your weak spots before the front office ever realizes you have them.

Teacher's Too Busy For Children

Yes, there are times when a teacher simply must work at her desk while students are in the room. That monthly report must be done early in the afternoon of that last day, or the district office must have some statistics before 10:00 and it's now 9:30. One effective way to handle this dilemma is by making a tape of your voice beforehand. It takes less time to prepare a tape than it does to grade sets of written busy work. Another way is to run a best row contest.

One teacher . . . two voices

Children love poetry. Like music, poetry must be heard to be appreciated. Who has the time? Always, more pressing subjects jam the docket. Prerecord poems from reading test . . . as you record, add personal comments when you tell children to turn a page. Place a small group of students around a table; each has his copy of the text. If the table is near your desk, you can ask your trouble-makers to come up and listen while you're working. These tapes can also be used by turning them on low while you're presenting a live lesson in another part of the room.

May day, May day, May day

A *best row* contest is good for 30 to 45 minutes, no more. Elicit best row qualifications from the class and list on board. Inform children you're keeping a tally at your desk while you complete work for the principal. From time to time you'll look up, and the best row *at that moment* will get a point. About midway they'll want to know which row is ahead. Be careful. To keep all rows competing, it needs to be a tight race. The prize? The glory of winning—a wrapped candy—extra recess time.

EIGHT RECOMMENDATIONS FOR STARTING THE YEAR

Interviewing literally dozens and dozens of outstanding teachers crystalized the following conclusions in my thinking. I offer them as a summary indicating the teachers' general professional opinions and recommendations on the task of establishing a natural control in the classroom.

1. Consider training-period time as an important investment. Your shakedown cruise for establishing methods, procedures and class rules should last the first several days. For this purpose use fascinating lesson subject matter, but don't worry if the children don't absorb it. In fact, don't bother with grades. If you grade at all, make it a ✓+ ✓ ✓- on the systems you're teaching. Completing orientation in a few days, then start year's studies in earnest and at the same time concertedly and positively teach conduct standards for two, four or six weeks, depending on your neighborhood. You may want to explain to the children some of the actions and attitudes required of you as a member of the faculty.

2. Set conduct standards and goals for the children. Make six or eight classroom rules—no more. Usually children enjoy making suggestions for these. Put many, many ideas on the board, and let the class choose those few they consider most important and fair.

3. Teach the six or eight rules to the children. Actively teach the rules to the students. Any way you want to do it is fine, but be sure you do more than hang a list on a bulletin board.

4. Privately, make a list of student antics which irk you. Don't worry whether they *should* bother you . . . if they do bother you now, put them down. Then, after you've completed you list, split it. Now you have two lists, one you might call Requires Attention and the other Ignore. You'll be smart to revise your list at the end of two weeks, and again at the end of a second two weeks. Growing children change, and so do progressive teachers.

Example:

Requires Attention	*Ignore*
Carrying weapons	No paper or pencil
Destroying property	Gum chewing
Fighting	Messy desks
Etc.	Etc.

5. Keep misdemeanor and its correction related. They're well related in your mind: just be sure that students see a pattern or relationship. Examples:

Loud talking–Supervised session in soft whispering.
Uncontrolled roaming–Confined to seat after school.
Careless direction following–Copy directions five or ten times.

In addition to this I would suggest always having a brief, remedially-inclined talk with a student concerning the offense.

6. Express salient qualities yourself. Every trait in which children need improving–start working on that trait in your duties and attitudes. For example: Class is lacking in consideration of others. Work on being considerate in your every contact, whether it seems important or not.

7. Balance every complaint with a compliment. This is an invaluable aid in helping one to avoid becoming a scold–or terribly discouraged–especially if one has a naughty or slow group. Every time you must correct a child, compliment that child (or another child) on an unrelated good feat. You'll catch them being good and doing intelligent things in lots of small ways which formerly escaped your attention. This helps to break the negative cycle.

8. Call children's homes regularly. About six calls on a Friday will get you through the average class in a month: A good report gives parents two days to praise and reward. A bad report gives them two days to work on correction of attitudes.

CONCLUSION

Healthy self respect and a true dominion in your outlook are the first steps in establishing an easy, consistent classroom atmosphere. They bring equipoise to your speech and action. As a professional group, teachers are prone to be both idealistic and domineering. Since domineering personalities usually feed on self-righteousness, remedial action involves learning to appreciate others. Wise aspirations, humility and gratitude fortify our efforts to appreciate and respect the innate rights of others, even very little folk.

Heighten your unique style of teaching by accenting, without apology, those things you do best. Blend your style with the character of classroom atmosphere for which you're stretching. Two ideal atmospheres from which to initiate further development of style are: Respect tinged with kindliness and kindliness tinged with respect. So much can be said for either case.

A key to an effective classroom community in discipline matters is an ability to decide wisely what is best for the child *within* the context of the group. Individual and group rights are not always in conflict; after all, each child has the need and the right to learn group living. Another verbal joust is the "immediate versus the long term welfare" of the child. It's not necessarily a choice between extremes; look again: there's often a middle fork in the road.

Here it is, one more time . . . . Clear your own thought of emotion before you handle a behavior incident.

Finally, quietly polishing your control techniques with systematic diligence is a clever way to improve your teaching results. No one needs to realize what you're doing. In the meantime you'll add noticable time and energy to your teaching day. Teaching day and classroom day are not necessarily terms to be equated, though often so used. Since you'll be training students in conduct for as many years as you teach, why not hone your analysis incisiveness, enlarge your technique repertoire and add a polish to your tact?

7 Solving Attendance and Related Problems

A red brick and stone fortress–the newer part completed in '93–it squatted glowering in a factory neighborhood predominately Slavic. As we stood in the central hallway with its dark woodwork, naked pipes, and extremely high ceiling, we could see the stair wells at either end. The teachers had their classes lined up on both sides of the stairs, waiting for the 2nd dismissal bell. Perfect patience. Perfect order. Perfect quiet. The newly-assigned principal looked at one end, then at the other; then she shuddered, and mumbled, "You know, at times I don't think I can take one more day of their docility."

Indeed, wasn't she a considerate person to feel the unnaturalness of thoroughly subdued children? And honest, for refusing to take pride in it? Let's take heart and remember her remark the next time our children charge into the school as if they're playing a new game called "Storming the Bastille." Of course, neither extreme is good. When children are naturally self-controlled there will still be a few wiggles, and kicks in the shin; but the general *tone* is orderly.

In this chapter, we'll consider the processes and problems related to the child's arrival and departure: tardiness, lockers, halls and stairs, absence, and dismissals. Making and enforcing general rules covering many of these situations are most valuable in lending a stability to the scene–until eventually some things "just aren't done in our school."

TARDINESS

Punctuality is a hallmark of consideration for others. Since it's a habit, and a habit which involves thinking ahead a little bit, learning to leave a leeway in time for the unexpected, it also helps anyone arrive at his destination with his wits more collected. In this age most of us need all the wits we can garner.

It's important that the class get off to a good start together each morning. Teachers will keep their thinking clearer if they remember, even when thoroughly exasperated, that insisting on school promptness has its greatest value in helping a child learn group feeling and *his rightful place* as a responsible member of the group.

Sometimes a child lives in a home where every member of the family is on a different schedule–or none at all. He has little opportunity to observe that some people consider time valuable. Thus, he most needs to be coached–maybe coaxed–into learning this fact of life. It will help him fit into the world as he'll find it–not as he would have it, not as we would have it, but as it is.

Whether shuffling down a crusty, fascinating alley or ambling through a meadow on his way to school, almost every child is accompanied by a little invisible fellow riding on his shoulder, the elf Curosity. School bells can seem very remote when this elf whispers, "Is that a baby chipmunk under the broken basket? No, stupid, it's a baby mouse. Let's follow him and see where he lives." Before you know it, our bigger friend is in trouble–he's late.

Here are some suggestions which gifted and sympathetic teachers have offered to share.

Little laddie, you're always late

Tardiness is a chronic affliction of his life? Send a note home. Ask the child to return it the following morning–signed. If it doesn't come back, send another note. If number two note doesn't come back immediately, phone the parents.

Formula: 4xT=40

T stands for tardy slip, 4 stands for the number of occasions you have given one to a particular student, and the 40 stands for a 40-minute make-up period before or after school.

This is the way the records read

Ditto tardy forms and let class secretary maintain records in a small file box. Caution: Don't attempt this until you have reasonable control of the group.

Date ____________	TARDY
Date ____________	
Date ____________	
Minutes Late ____________	
Reason ______________________________	
	Signed ____________ Student

Mission: escort

Kennie lived nearby but he was always late, and often he claimed his mother was responsible. Soon the classroom teacher started to check the playground at 8:50. If Kennie was not at school, she called his home. If he had left, she sent a dependable child to the corner to meet him and hustle him on to school. She sent the second child to a corner she was able to see from her classroom window, and consequently the second child was not off school grounds unsupervised.

The courtesy of kings

As constructive punishments for a chronically tardy student, please consider some of the following:

1. Have him make a list of interesting occupations which require either promptness or an acute sense of timing. A few examples . . . . a dynamite expert, newspaper reporter, jet pilot, astronaut, TV actor, movie stunt man. He may use library books or an encyclopedia. A book on vocations is another good source. Twenty-five is a very long list.
2. Have him describe to you on paper or tape the exact role timing plays in a job calling for precision arrivals and departures. For example: How important is timing in the

work of a TV star in the youngster's favorite program. What would be the results if the star showed up ten minutes after the program was on camera.

3. Have him write a one-page paper on tape a two minute spiel on Greenwich Time, or on life in the United States before time zones were established.
4. Have him tell you what might happen to a counterspy who arrived ten minutes late for a secret rendezvous.
5. He's an international pilot careless about a few minutes here and a few minutes there. As a result he runs 15 minutes short on fuel over the ocean, and must ditch his airplane. Have him look up ditching and tell you about it.

DAWDLING AT LOCKERS

Nuisance locker problems tend to disappear as children grow older. Briefly, kindly remarks by an older person in charge, combined with one of the following actions, usually speed up the performance naturally.

Locker lockout

Most of the class has learned the rules, but a few children are still slamming doors, dawdling or fighting. Deny them their lockers for a short time. Have them keep coats, mufflers, rubbers and mittens at their seats. Insist they not bother other children by allowing their personal belongings to spread or scatter.

On your mark . . . . get set

One day keep locker dawdlers in at recess. Using a timer, let them practice coat-hat-boot routine.

Aye, aye sir, right away

Make the dawdler a line captain, front or rear, instead of scolding him. Still another dawdler? Make him holder of the door.

Please teacher–a little more time?

Think it over carefully. Sometimes the kindest way of coping with dawdling is to let the slow poke go to his locker ahead of the class.

Beneath a watchful eye

For wee dawdlers, send them to lockers to get coats and boots. Have them bring clothing into the room and put it on near your desk.

The girls we left behind

Sometimes the best thing in the world is simply to leave the dawdlers behind—especially at recess.

ABSENCES

Particularly among younger children you may find a few students who have "tummy aches" and other semi-authentic reasons for staying home frequently. You may feel the home errs on the side of protectiveness, but you rarely can say anything, at least directly.

Excessive absence is most likely to show up among children who are not succeeding. Sometimes lack of success brings on lack of interest, and at other times lack of interest brings on lack of success. The first priority for long-range correction is to fortify the child's confidence, insisting that he learn to do something well. One immediate step which may interest you is to casually and sincerely remind him of his loss due to a doubtful absence. Perhaps, when talking to the class about yesterday's movie, add, "Oh, that's right, Ichabod, you missed it. I'm sorry you didn't get to see it." Naturally you're not going to rub it in if you really think a child was sick; but these remarks, consistently made, help the vague, timid cases.

Most schools have well-defined practices for handling absences, but here are a few ideas teachers have offered for your consideration.

Date ______________________ ABSENCE

Day absent ________________

Reason ____

____

Written excuse from home Yes ________ No ________

Signed ______________________

Student

At last she's got something to do

The class secretary maintains absence records in a file box. Ditto some forms and turn them over to her. Let her remind the children about bringing written excuses.

Absence makes the heart grow fonder

Tell your wandering, class-cutting friends that you missed them and you want to get to know them better. They now have an invitation to your very exclusive Breakfast Club. Since they are expected to be prompt for this social event, ask them to arrive in the morning at the same time as you do. Inasmuch as they missed out on an earlier feast of knowledge, let them make up the time studying.

French leave?

You suspect the absent student is truant. Call his home. If he's not there, ask the home not to mention your call. When he returns to school, ask him for an explanation. If he tells the truth, apply sanctions mildly. If he lies, take firmer action.

Swapping one hour for another

If a child cuts class within a week or so of an all-school extra event, keep him in the classroom on the special day. Explain to him that you are cutting into his time because he cut out on class time—but he is paying the additional price of missing all school fun. Naturally, good judgment would prevent you from causing a child to miss a once-a-year event dear to his heart, such as a track meet for a youngster who's keen on track.

HALLS AND STAIRS

Halls tell the atmosphere of a school—so say some experts. During the day children get in and out of halls from classrooms, so passing periods between classes provide good clues. If, at the end of a period, students burst out of a room like the lid coming off a steam kettle, they have probably been under tension in the classroom and little learning was taking place. If they amble and scuffle out, they have most likely been learning.

Many teachers like to stand at the door and greet students as they arrive; and their principals are still keener for them to do it. It's a good time to notice the condition of the students, and to adjust to them if they are arriving tense. There are three different ways you can handle a tense-on-arrival class. One, let them chatter for a few minutes. Two, talk to them yourself. That is, talk about something not related to your subject or the day's work. Keep on talking until you sense a calmed-down attitude. The third, and best: make a humorous remark which gets them laughing. Laughter breaks tension quickly and surely.

Here are a few suggestions teachers made when I questioned them about halls and stairs. In several cases you'll notice the remark lifts the exhortation from a reprimand to a friendly reminder.

Pre-empt their position

As you meet a group of students horsing around in the hall, try, "I hate this school. I can't even walk down the lousy hall without someone bothering me." You've taken favorite words right out of their mouths. Momentarily, and only momentarily, they're speechless. Then they'll usually start chattering, and will cooperate actionwise.

Cozy cuddling

A boy-girl combination is too close for good taste. Speak to the boy: "If I take the girl's fingerprints, I don't want to get yours." That's all the hint they usually need.

We have only your welfare in mind, sir

Stop a running youngster. In mock seriousness ask him if his Blue Cross is paid. Lightheartedly, give him a royal explanation: you've discontinued stopping youngsters because of school rules. Now it's only their health and welfare you're concerned about.

Down the stairs at 18 knots

Knotted rope makes a great training aid for teaching primary and middle grade children how to form and keep straight lines evenly spaced and paced. It is also useful for getting these children across the streets safely.

Example: You have 18 boys and 23 girls in the room. Take two lengths of rope. In one put 18 knots at the intervals you want the boys spaced in; likewise 23 knots in the other. Every time the children line up, have them use the rope as a spacer. During the early weeks of your training have them walk in and out of the building, each child holding his knot.

Early though, start testing their progress. Step one would be to use the rope to line the class up, and then to leave the rope in the room. Step two would be testing the children to line up evenly—no squeezing or butting—without using the rope.

A field trip suggestion: Before your outing, let the children choose partners for the day. Each pair of students put their names on a tag and choose a knot in the rope at which to tie their tag. Then when you're at the zoo or wherever, and need to have the children line up, time is shortened and minor hassles are eliminated; yet the children don't feel dictated to. You probably would want to break your class into four or five squads and use four or five ropes; and thus you can see immediately who's missing.

Student Hall Guards

About the only two types of student hall guard systems are the stationary and the roving. The roving hall guard squad can be much smaller (e.g., 3 or 4 students per period for a junior high school enrollment of 800) than the stationary guard. Naturally, the rovers are free to ferret students out of favorite building hideaways—which change as quickly from week to week as the staff learns about them. However, one drawback, the roving squad is constantly being challenged by teachers who don't realize which youngsters are on duty for that period. Sometimes badges or arm bands are satisfactory.

The stationary crew is larger (e.g., eight or ten students per period for an enrollment of 800). These students can be a greater help to visitors, and class-cutting students know for sure that they will be challenged in certain areas. In either system it is most wise to assign teachers during lunch period, when traffic is heavy.

Naturally, in most schools guards have earned the privilege of office through their own good citizenship. One excellent plan is to choose them on a yearly basis, but then switch their duty periods at the semester break. This balances out the individual student's schedule.

BATHROOM AND FOUNTAIN

Although the term bathroom recess started out as a euphemism, many children have adroitly revamped the session into an accurate phrase—they get into bathrooms and play. One thing you'll notice is that if bathroom recess comes after outdoor recess, the children sometimes fiddle and fool around and it takes them 15 minutes. Try taking the class to the bathroom five minutes before outdoor recess. While the weather is nice, this works well to speed things up.

Here are a number of ways different teachers have learned to handle bathroom and drinking-fountain requests.

When there is no group-going-to-the-bathroom break, cards can effectively control traffic. Have one marked "B" and the other "G." Place these on a front ledge. When a child leaves the classroom, he simply turns a card over. Never more than one girl and one boy are out of the room at a given time. When the cards are not out on the ledge, it means there is no bathroom privilege for anyone. These times include one hour after school has started, morning and afternoon, during important lessons, group discussions and tests.

Let's count the number of minutes

You hear a little voice asking, "May I go to the bathroom? May I get a drink of water?" Is it a real need? Say pleasantly, "Yes, you may go, but you'll have to make up the time you are out of the room." Many inquirers then change their minds about the trip. Still, you haven't said No. Almost always, there'll be a few children for whom you'll have to make the decision.

Boys go in the door marked BOYS

This seems like nonsense to some children for at home everyone uses the same bathroom. So, if a youngster tries to peek into the girls' washroom, you have to handle it; but treat it lightly. You might ask him to write a paragraph on why his school needs a supply of boys' hair bows. This way you're not making a federal case of an incident which well could have been done in an impish mood, yet the girls feel you have "done something" about the unwelcome visitor.

For your friends, count slowly

Assign a child to hold drinking fountain handle for the others. Have him count to three while each child drinks. In hot weather increase the count to ten.

Two by two

If you don't give the class a group bathroom break, send pairs to the bathroom and then for a long drink. If a child is disobedient, he may go only at special times for a week, two weeks, or a month. These special times are when you're taking the class somewhere–for example, to an assembly.

DISMISSAL

Time to go home! As early as 1919 some thoughtful educators were objecting to the "outmoded" practice of lining children up by room membership when they are leaving or entering the building. Certainly we can follow the humanity of their reasoning, though in some schools we must realize the impracticality of the total freedom–chaos?–which their advice implies. In government we have concepts of pure democracy and of politics, the art of the possible; in schools, along with concepts of pure and maximum development of the individual, we must have professional realism, the art of the possible for a given set of circumstances.

Since the mechanics of arrival and dismissal are most important in the lower and middle years, most of the suggestions included are pointed towards those age groups. However, you'll also find some excellent information on dismissing a class row by row in these pages; this is applicable for any age group at any time of day.

Casual style or formal line? If a teacher sincerely objects to regimenting children, it would seem wise for her to thoughtfully consider the overall picture and her alternatives. Children need a continuity of ground rules from year to year. Thus, if the majority of her colleagues believe in line-ups, surely she can find the flexibility to go along with the consensus of opinion. In such a case the children would welcome her explanation of her personal convictions and why she is yielding to the will of the group.

Here are some suggestions for handling the flurry which occurs in most school rooms near bell time. You'll notice that the strength of these suggestions lies in their very obviousness.

Can't you hear anything, teacher?

Don't nag about noise the last few minutes of the school day. Once or twice, ask the children to be quiet. Still noisy? Go to your desk and start marking papers. Show no concern over conditions; but when the bell rings, ignore it. Soon your pupils will worry and ask about leaving. Explain that they must be quiet for three, four, or five minutes before you'll give permission.

Keep it under your hat

Ask children to put important notes and notices under their caps, in their mittens or in their boots.

Safe–sure–simple

Several papers are to go home today? Fold them in half and staple them together, or ask a student helper to do so. This way a child won't drop one paper, maybe even while crossing a street, and turn around and go back for it.

Going-home groups

Divide the children into groups according to the direction from school in which they live . . . bus children in one corner, children who cross at the red light in another, and so on. Have children fetch their coats and boots from lockers and then sit in their groups to put them on.

Less time for fumbling . . . more time for fun

Send a letter to each home about the importance of proper outer clothing. Most parents are eager to help, and if they cooperate on this aspect it will in turn add about 15 minutes a day to the school activities schedule. Primary level.

Dear Parents,

Winter is fast approaching and you are probably getting out the snow boots, pants, etc. This is a good time to have practice sessions at home before the first big snowfall.

A child needs patience and practice in learning to coordinate. Does your child need to know about zippers at the bottom cuff of the snow pants? Does he understand about pulling it over the heel of his shoe? Does he know how to pull his boots on over his regular school shoes?–how to fasten the boots?–how to take off his boots alone?–quickly?

There are still mittens, hats, caps, sweaters, and scarves unmarked. Please help us keep the children's outfits intact.

Thank you very much for your cooperation.

The Primary Teachers

Line-up

Instead of asking children to be quiet, consider giving them something on which to focus attention. Along the wall where the children line up, and at child's eye level, place lone cardboard strips which have on them unusual magazine or newspaper pictures. Rarely do the children line up in the same order, so they'll find those pictures interesting for a week or two. CAUTION: Use paste and the children won't fiddle with the display. If you tack up the material, your carefully chosen pictures won't prove as stimulating to the imaginative as a fresh source of pins.

Footsteps from behind

May not be mysterious, but the children know they're being watched. In dismissal procedure let a student captain do the leading. This frees you to gather the dawdlers and forgetters of treasured trinkets and needed books, and to close the door. The journey to the outside world should be broken into sections. The cardinal rule for segment length is, "How far can you, the teacher, see?" Instruct the line captain, "Lead the children to the end of the hall and wait." When you catch up then say, "Lead the children down one flight of stairs and wait until I give you the next signal." Etc.

Paradise lost and regained

Through misconduct a child has lost recess privilege and yet you have yard duty. Take him out with you and have him sit and watch the others play—and then for the last five minutes, let him play, too. The playtime will be more precious to him, and he does need the exercise.

CONCLUSION

The mechanics of getting children in and out of the classroom, bathroom, and building hold their greatest importance only in the aspect that when they are smoothly done they increase the time and energy available for more rewarding pursuits. The mundane is kept to a minimum.

The chronic habit of tardiness in an individual can be costly to him in later years, but it's also costly in time—to the class—right now. Rarely is it a deep-seated thing. Many are the imaginative ways for correcting this tendency.

The next facet we considered was absence, especially excessive absence. In our attempts to alleviate it we must first look for underlying reasons, because this problem can be dissolved only at the source. Usually it's intimately connected with lack of success in school work.

Halls are a good barometer of a school and the amount of genuine learning which is taking place. Almost every experienced teacher and educator can accurately size up a building the minute he opens the front door.

In many schools children have taken us at our own level of terminology, and have made bathroom recess a second play period. Soon, perhaps someone will think of a more apt name.

Dismissal procedures are not traditional (regimented) and modern (casual) only because of the preference of the staff. Usually the staff's thinking considers the total environment of the school and neighborhood, and tries to do what is best for all concerned. Here again, fine suburban schools can and should extend a casual freedom to the children because such freedom really fits the setting. These children's parents have prepared their children for handling the increased freedom.

8 Communications Problem-- Oral and Written

Children continue to be interested in each other, with or without adult approval. Sometimes they talk at awkward, wrong times, too. Not only that, they've been known to express unwelcome ideas in even more unwelcome, vivid terms. This chapter deals with a few communication problems and some workable ideas on how to alleviate them.

Not the university pundits, nor the curriculum coordinators, nor the principals, nor the prophets sitting under a banyan tree, but the outstandingly adept teachers themselves, told me repeatedly this major rule: Trouble of every sort can best be prevented by getting each school day off to a good start. They advised being systematic in a casual way, getting things ready the afternoon before, if necessary. Twenty minutes' preparation brings huge returns, more like a stock split than stock dividends.

Listen afresh for the pattern and content of children's speech. Brevity is the keynote—except when they want to tell one of their longwinded stories—which you don't want to take the time for—and don't want to hear, particularly—and you know ahead of time—that it will be all tedious details and no plot—with plenty of repetition—and then there will be a flashback or two which isn't needed—and by this time you wonder when will the thing ever end—and then the storyteller takes a deep breath—and finally you say, "Please, I'll give you two minutes to finish the story."

A child may have similar feelings about a teacher's longwindedness, but students can't set deadlines for educators. So you see that if a teacher is prone to "much speaking," it presents a real communications problem for a child. Many of us, children or otherwise, find it difficult to keep friendly talks and reprimands degassed.

Is there such a thing as a perfect correction? I believe there is, and one for every predicament. How to find it?

Obviously, the first step is to listen. Listen to the child's reasons for talking or acting as he did. Then offer your response or correction in a friendly voice. With both children and adults, the perfect chiding refines and sharpens the erring one's perception of a mistake and at the same time strengthens his understanding of a right or a better way. Squelches are out of bounds *since a good rebuke makes its point without offending.* A perfect correction can be very brief. Indeed, like wit, it should be brief.

Words, however, may need reinforcing by sanctions. For example, denial of a privilege or of a freedom may be a part of your total action. Brief withholding and then restoration of a privilege, repeated if necessary, is best.

The following material is directed toward helping you unobtrusively handle, the mundane task of gaining and keeping everyone's interest. As the tone of the room becomes purposeful, and the noise level rather well under control, your time and energy are freed for better teaching, and for handling serious behavior matters with greater thoughtfulness and aplomb.

NOISY ROOM–CORRECTION BY COMMENT, SIGNAL, AND ACTION

Lilt, and a ken for introducing surprise flourishes, are always welcome in a teaching personality. With-it comments, witty quips, the topical touch, all add variety in gathering the groups' attention. New phrases have a surprise element which snags attention and at the same time lessens any for-the-3,000th-time-be-quiet tone in your voice.

One device for bolstering an element of humor and the unexpected turn is placing a different witty quotation of some famous man on the board daily. Building a feel for imagination and whimsy, these can help cut the idea many children get that goodness and hard working people are by their very natures dull. Don't use quotes that openly moralize; youngsters get plenty of moralizing from other sources.

Some admired teachers suggested the following techniques for the ever-present chore of attracting the group's attention.

Shhhh . . . . your favorite teacher wants to say something

Start softly, "I've got a secret." A few will listen. Again, "I've got a secret." A few more will respond. The third time you will have the entire class. Then tell them one fact–something about the house you live in, your tame rhino, themselves (all people are astounding), or whatever.

Shhhh . . . I hear the good fairy

A good fairy whispered in your ear, and you want to share it. Repeat. Inform children the good fairy told you her plan. She will go around room and tap the shoulder of each good boy and girl. When they've been tapped, pupils are to signal you by sitting up. You might add, "Once upon a time the fairy not only tapped each child, but she gave one child a pair of golden shoes." Watch them check their own feet, no one else's. Useful with primary grades

Couldn't be more simple

One quietly outstanding teacher suggested her most effective device. Put your finger to your lips and smile. That's it. That's all she does.

Cock your ears, little flock

Whisper directions. You'll have to repeat two or three times, but keep on whispering . . . even to the "OK, go ahead with your work."

Shhh . . . which of us is out of step?

Ask your class, "Am I crabby today, or are you unusually noisy?" Students like this approach, and respond well.

Some of the devices listed under Changing Subjects, page 169, are also helpful.

When you use spoken comments in attracting a class's attention, variety is a keystone, chaps. However, an action or an audible signal provokes the best response when it's a recognized symbol. One suggestion: you might like to try several different types and let your class vote on the one they like best.

Peace, peace, that is peace

Teach a hand signal which means "peace." When you, the room president, or a person leading a discussion raises his hand in this signal, everyone is to be quiet.

According to my watch

Hold your watch arm up and obviously study the face. At the same time announce, "It's now 10:32. How long will it take to get everyone's attention?" Keep on looking at your watch. One child will nudge another. After initial training the class responds well and quickly. Later, you'll need only to raise your wrist.

Tinkle, tinkle

Ring a small bell when class is noisy. Warning: Don't use the bell as both a subject-switch signal and a noise reducer.

Noise Room–Action

Ball one, ball two, ball three . . .

During a silent period, students start talking. First offense: Have them tell class what they were talking about. Second offense: Have each write a 100 word note explaining not only what he was talking about, but why. This is a big task for a fifth or sixth grader. Third offense: Have each write the same type of note and you read it to class.

No ship's bell

What is it you need to save your voice when your classroom is unusually noisy? Take a pair of scissors and rap them against a metal object. The sound is sharp enough to alert everyone. This device will wear out if used too often.

Your room is all a fluster

And your benign requests for order are being totally ignored. Ask several of your flighty students each to write a letter. This may be addressed either to a well-liked homeroom teacher whose esteem they value, or–in serious cases–to a principal whose esteem they must have. Each student merely explains his reasons *why* it's not reasonable to expect him to obey your requests and directions, or to begin the task at hand. As the children start writing, the entire atmosphere of the room ripples into tranquility–usually. Deliver the letters, or not, according to the way the child has acted during the balance of the period.

. . . . Room in purgatory

Keep three or four seats vacant near your desk or in the front of the room. When you have a persistent mischief-maker, have him bring his books and take a place near you. Thus, you can keep an eye on him, and at the same time easily and quietly extend encouraging remarks. If he redeems himself, he may return to his assigned seat the next day. Generally speaking, allow him no more than three days in which to purge himself of his conspicuous offenses . . . then send him to your school's limbo. Do notice, teacher, that by inference, heaven is defined as an assigned seat in your classroom.

Don't fight 'em, join 'em

Occasionally an entire room will decide to heckle a teacher on a given signal–say, coughing at 2:05 sharp. End the contest–maybe–by coughing along with them.

Disaster has struck

Perhaps conditions have gone from bad to total chaos and you have lost all control of the room. Tell class to stand, and to stand still. Choose a boy to be minute-counter by watching the clock. Inform group it will stay after school one minute for every minute it takes them to settle. If necessary, keep them after school.

Though this approach is not fair, it may be the fairest thing you can do when the general atmosphere is so totally up for grabs and squirming that you can't pick the offenders.

It's the taxpayers' money

Taxpayers want teachers to teach. Explain to children that the school board hired you for a specific job. During school hours the students' conduct must allow you to teach without unreasonable distraction. If their conduct interferes with your assignment, then you must keep them after school to fulfill your responsibility to the taxpayers. If you must resort to this step, it will be done at your convenience.

How long will these sessions be? Here's a good pattern. Let's say you have a noisy room at 8:56. Write that number on the board. Stand quietly until you have order. If it takes until 8:58, put a number 2 in the upper corner of the board. Repeat during the day whenever necessary. If time does add up to about 15 minutes, keep them after school.

In this case no athletic event or religious training obligation excuses an individual. Remind children you will be glad to talk to displeased parents about your decision. Usually, one session after school handles the problem for the remainder of the year. After that, all you'll need do is write the time on board, and the room will calm down.

NOISY INDIVIDUALS–COMMENTS AND ACTIONS

While correcting noisy children, especially when dealing with them as individuals, it's always wise to remember that one of a child's basic aims is a place in the group. Emphasize, with genuine conviction, the reality of his *special* place. Of course, you would not threaten, belittle, or in any way jeopardize that place.

Occasionally the kindest action you can take is to isolate the noise one quickly, but remind him that his vacant niche is waiting for him while he's gone. Incidentally, your purpose in sending him out of the room is to teach him not to distract others. You have no desire to humiliate him. Thus it would be only considerate to see that he has something to sit on besides his haunches–perhaps his own desk chair, a cushion, or even a hassock.

Frequently children's out-of-turn talking can be lessened or eliminated by simpler steps–some are almost incredibly simple actions. First, the teacher may want to try just looking at the child and shaking her head No. Or, without using facial expression, she may walk over to the child and stand there all the while continuing with her original lesson subject. Then, if this doesn't stop it, she may want to put a hand on his shoulder. (This is especially effective for repeat offenders if the teacher walks down an inside aisle–where teachers don't often walk.)

Another simple thing she can do is to interject a quiet reminder. For instance, she might be talking about astronauts and saying "During their final orbit around the moon . . . no, Johnny, cut it out . . . the astronauts were . . . . " Here an important feature is to use the same tone of voice for the whole sentence.

Two violinists playing the same score of Brahms can give entirely different experiences to the audience. The notes are only symbols of sound; the depth, the majesty, must be conveyed by the performer and received differently by each listener. So it is with the suggestions offered by highly skilled teachers I interviewed, the printed symbol of procedure is here; but you must add the artistry, the perceptive warmth which will inspire each different student or group.

Many fine teachers told me they always offer a chatterbox a choice of alternatives. Examples: "Do you want to quit talking, or shall I give you an assignment during your free period?" or "Which do you prefer, to take a seat in the rear of the room, or to stay after school?" Obviously, the teacher is being less arbitrary, less bossy in the children's eyes.

Perhaps this is the moment to mention the reactions of students whom I interviewed on the subject of discipline. Without exception they approved of the teacher who "did something," who didn't just talk things over or lecture them. Since this view is so contrary to the accepted practice, which aims at evolving gradual attitude-change in youngsters through counseling, the only solution I can offer is to do both. Have a short talk with the child and then assign a simple physical inconvenience, so that you have "done something" from the child's viewpoint.

Here are some suggested comments which splendid teachers considered appropriate when students are talking at inconvenient times.

We're waiting

Say, "We're waiting" in a soft, friendly tone for great effectiveness.

A marked man

With your finger make a large X on the student's back while he's talking. Use a friendly, kidding tone and tell him, "Now you're a marked man." Most often he'll like this hint and take the warning.

Scholarly inquiry . . . . . mebbe

In mock seriousness say, for example, "I know you two are discussing profound academic matters, but unless you can manage a more scholarly pose, I must ask you to stop." Most often youngsters will smile and turn to their tasks. Sometimes, they'll try stroking chins and shaking heads sagely. This could be your cue to nod approval, adding something like, "That's impressive, but not impressive enough."

The price of being a man

Literally for a few boys only, but with good judgment it can be applied far more often than seems likely at first. Tell lads, "You probably don't realize how far your heavy, masculine voices carry." Even when they know they're being flattered, they love it.

. . . . and to the capricious clown

Quietly tell him, "If you clown, I'll scold. If you think your antics are so delightful that the class will overlook my scolding, go ahead and entertain them. If you think they'll resent listening to me nag, save your fun for later." (This approach was offered by a teacher who has been nationally honored for his ability to inspire young people.)

What did you use for bait, sir?

To separate heads of whispering students, ask them, "Have I ever told you about the big fish I caught?" Put your hands between their heads and simultaneously say, "It was that long," as you push their heads apart. Greatly appeals to most roughneck boys.

Conduct out of line?

Pull his chair a little out of line. If he wants to be earmarked as a little different, accommodate him. This gesture is mild and it's effective at all grade levels.

From one loud mouth to another

Assign a very noisy student to work with an equally noisy child about three years his grade junior. Older child is amazed that anyone so little can be so noisy. It helps both children.

Congress has a gag rule

But here you are in a schoolroom and that child's mouth is never, never closed. There's a roll of masking tape in your desk–but resist the temptation. Safer action: Cut two pieces of tape. Write anything from "prithee, fair maiden/no prittle prattle," to "Cut the yak/Jack." Apply a piece to each of the student's hands, or wrap his thumbs. If you speak kindly and softly while you're doing this, you have a chance, teacher.

Your ID card, please

Warn unruly students. Then 1) Ask for ID cards. Explain you plan to keep cards for the rest of the period. 2) If they settle down, you'll return cards. If they don't, you'll turn cards in to the office (or homeroom, etc.) Upper grades.

Yon is main office

You have a normally well-behaved child who's been slipping. Private talks and calls to his home have not revealed a reason for the change. One day ask him to stay in at recess and then, since you must first take care of an errand to the office, have him meet you at a landmark near the office. Mention no names. Make no threats. Just tell him the spot you've chosen would be a convenient place to discuss your differences. Most children will get the message without a single word of direct reference from you.

THE CURSE ON 200 SENTENCES

For as long as anyone can remember, educators have been sniffing with displeasure at the idea of assigning students the task of writing 100, 200, or 500 sentences. Yet many excellent teachers and administrators have been continuing to assign the sentence-writing task. Perhaps the major reason for their disregard of the curse on 200 sentences is that no one has told them of a better way which does not involve more than a little of their time; and their time can be incredibly precious on the very day a youngster decides to act the scamp. Intuitively, perhaps, teachers recognize that the argument against sentence-writing is not total. There is also a case for sentence-writing.

I respectfully submit that sentence-writing in moderation does not have the pernicious influence of many other sanctions commonly used in correcting children. To name one such practice: nagging.

Through the centuries English advocates and magistrates, engaged in legal trials among a most law-abiding people, have emphasized the urgency of reaching for an underlying sense of fairnesss . . . Equally important, according to their thinking, is the swiftness and sureness of correction–not the severity. And it is widely recognized that the English highly cherish individuality in all walks of life.

As you probably noted, the key points above are: sense of fairness, swiftness and sureness of correction, and a respect for individuality. Now let's tie these in with the sentence-writing task. In assigning very moderate sentence tasks, it's relatively easy for an extremely busy teacher to be fair, and more important, to seem fair in the child's eyes. Also, she can attend to the situation immediately when it should be handled, for she knows that it will not consume a lot of her time.

The next point: the assignment is definite, and it requires energy and action on the child's part. This is an action which expunges. He has now paid for breaking the rules and *he* knows it. He does not owe a debt of gratitude to an "understanding" counseling teacher whom he may or may not like, and who may or may not like him. Understanding can operate both ways. Of course a child doesn't recognize that he "understands" his teachers–he merely sizes them up.

The case against sentence-writing tasks is all too apparent, for it incurs the dullness of rote and foolish repetition. In some fine suburban schools a teacher need never resort to assigning sentences. She has too many things going for her: a good atmosphere, relatively small classes, cooperative parents, and students in whose homes tactful reasoning is normal.

In other schools other teachers must work with large classes of deprived children from difficult–often irrational–homes. Inevitably, and rightly, teachers make lots of allowances for the children, in learning and deportment, in tardiness and truancy. Teachers know that the students come from homes where physical punishment is the primary way in which parents correct–action punishment and not reasoning punishment.

In such schools the teachers are not working in a Dick and Jane world, so let's quit giving them feelings of guilt and inferiority by smugly reminding them that their correction methods do not measure up to the perfection portrayed in educational methods courses.

Instead, let's forthrightly recognize that teachers in industrial and inner cities often simply cannot give the personalized attention which students need and deserve. In choosing deterrents, these hardship-post teachers and administrators must settle for the possible rather than the ideal and strive for fairness and moderation. These are honorable goals. Writing sentences can be a very moderate and fair, though terribly dull, reminder that society values order above most other virtues. And rightly. In chaos, both fairness and moderation disappear.

Two hundred time I won't

Tell the child that you recognize what a bore and time-waster it is to write 200 versions of "I will not do so-and-so." But he has forced you to choose, and you think you've chosen the lesser of two evils. Writing sentences, he wastes only his own time. Talking or horsing around, he wastes several persons' time.

TATTLING

Tattling is often done to hurt: the child who tells of another's small indiscretion wants to rejoice while the second one is being punished. Prevalent in second grade, tattling tends to disappear in the middle years and then it has an upsurge in the upper grades. Early in the school year have a talk with the class about possible exceptions to the rule of *not* reporting minor misdeeds by others. Your explanation about sincere desire to help the teacher and one another can do much to clarify the atmosphere. One widely acclaimed teacher told me she always emphasizes in her overall training of students the wonderful asset of self-control. Then when a child tattles on another, she has a short, quiet talk with him about the glorious quality of self-control.

Several remarkably talented teachers offered the following steps to curb this annoying, petty nuisance.

Tattle tail

Obtain or make a yarn tail. String on it little tags labeled Tattle Tail. Hang this tail on a bulletin board. If a child makes a nuisance report, direct his attention to the tail.

Inane information

Make a list of ten or 12 tattles you have received. Take a few minutes and read them all out. Just hearing the whole bunch of them usually effects a permanent cure for the entire class. Other people's tattle touch on no emotional sensitive spot to the listener, so he sees the tattles as the foolishness they are.

Please don't fetch my ear trumpet

As the tattler starts, put your fingers to your ears, smile, and shake your head.

Classify and reclassify crime

Explain to your young friend there are far more terrible misdeeds in the world than what her crony just did. Then with a smiling voice tell her that one of these is being a tattler.

SWEARING

Society draws numerous lines, and makes many erasures in the boundaries of vocabulary which is considered respectable or in good taste. Many adults are no longer always sure of what's in and what's out. How can the child be? More than anything be needs a rule of thumb, a guidance guage applicable to all occasions.

His best gauge is a discerning judgment of his own. You might tell your student that a major mark of a sharp person is his ability to choose the right words for a setting. Different circumstances–different ways of talking.

Perhaps you'll want to add one big purpose of his going to school is to learn new vocabulary. Most of these new words he can use anywhere, a few he'll need only for school or work. Safe ground: a metropolitan daily paper is a fine guide to acceptable usage. It includes slang and excludes the extreme. When in doubt, a child can ask himself the question, "Would I see these words in the hometown paper?"

If you're working with children whose cultural background permits greater lenience in language standards than your own, be sensitive in your consideration for a youngster's feelings of loyalty to his family, friends, and neighbors. Elude the trap of self-righteousness. Your views will then be more readily accepted, for you haven't indirectly set up critical judgment of your students' homes and buddies. In some neighborhoods you may want to explain that there is "home" talk and "school" talk. And you'll be helping all students, of all colors, accept Shakespeare and modern writers, playwrights and novelist with greater aplomb and better judgment.

Current literature notwithstanding, one large group of very professional teachers adopted the following basic rule for their school. They would individually accept and expect the same language in their classrooms that they would accept and expect in their private homes. Of course there will be differences from teacher to teacher but it would be up to the child to adjust. This stand was taken after they had collectively considered aspects of intent to insult, child's background, current plays and literature and their own moral convictions.

Here are several suggestions which were contributed by teachers who are with the modern world but not necessarily of it.

Cussin' and fussin'

Talk with the youngster about the reasons why people swear: frustrations, indignation, anger, the wish to show off or appear tough. Swear words are a poverty of expression. Assign to the cusser the task of looking up ten replacement words in a thesaurus. Have him keep this list at his desk.

Paper dragon teeth

Ask a child to compose a few paragraphs on why and on what occasions he finds swearing necessary.The essay makes an excellent basis for initiating a talk with him.

Bravado and a roccaco facade

Have the child write a definition of each word used. More often than not you'll learn he doesn't know the real meaning. Again, the written work makes an excellent basis for initiating a talk with him.

Cuss box

If student feels an urge to swear, he's to write the word and put it in a cuss box. Children offered this idea.

Could be valid, could be valid

Suggest to your friend that instead of swearing that he invent one, two, or three personal expletives and use these to vent exasperation.

One final bit of advice. All of us learn language by parroting others and swearing is just as contagious as slang. If the children who swear are not pressured to stop, other children who formerly didn't swear will start it.

HONESTY–LYING

Children rarely lie in the precise adult sense of the word. We all enjoy the sparkle of their imagination and the lucidity and candor of their preferences. When questioned, the lads and lassies in our classrooms merely tell the story as they see it. Only they usually just see their own side of the story.

Any time you require more information about an event which needs further discussion, ask three eyewitnesses to tell their versions. Fit these together. If you can, then act.

As you question students, try to phrase your inquiries in a fashion which avoids cornering the child or backing him against a wall.

Here are some more pertinent suggestions:

In Calhoun County we took a liar and . . . . . .

You expect to be faced with conflicting stories of an incident. During the preliminary interviewing, try to keep the individuals apart. 1) Talk to each student separately. 2) Have them meet as a group. 3) Ask the ones you trust most to speak first and repeat their stories. 4) Finally, ask the person whose word you doubt, "What is your comment?" If there's a discrepancy between his two accounts, dismiss the others and talk to him privately.

Maybe some teachers believe everything

You don't. Plainly tell liars, "You haven't told me the truth. We'll talk about this after school." Honest respect for their feelings and their need for privacy often brings far better results.

Call the shots as you see them

If you are *absolutely* sure a student is lying, say in front of the entire class, "You are lying to me, and though I now respect you, if you continue to lie I will lose respect for you."

NAME CALLING

Most often rampant name-calling is dissolved quickly by counseling the target child. Naturally you'll be sympathetic with his plight; and if you know of an ugly similar episode where the scapegoat won in the long run, tell him about it. In the meantime advise him not to react, or at least not to show his reactions. This way he'll take the punch out of the heckling.

If the child is suffering acutely from being called names, advise him to inform his tormentors, "You're making me angry enough I could hit you"—ask him not to whap offenders. Instead, let him come to you. Since they're pitting their combined strength against him, it is manly for him to gather more strength on his side. And on another angle would be to express some compliments privately about the scapegoat child to his tormentors.

Here is an entirely different way of handling scapegoatism—smoother, but not so deep cutting in getting at the cause of the problem.

Suddenly, one day, you become aware that the class is making a scapegoat of some child. A subtle counterattack can bring the swiftest solution. Say nary a word to the ringleaders; rather take an opportunity in class to quote a coach's or another teacher's praise of the scapegoat. Repeat the compliment(s) as often as is necessary, but make sure the class realizes that some well-liked authority respects the one whom they blame or bully. The bullying and blaming dissolve, usually.

In helping your class realize that name-calling is a facet of scapegoatism, here is a splendid vehicle you may want to try. Once you have it going, it offers many other useful possibilities.

After THAT day . . . well

Guide your youngsters in planning for the arrival of two infamous characters, two fictitious newcomers, to your room. Endow them with vivid personalities and christen them with descriptive names. Next set an enrollment date. On that day you may want to come up with large mâché models and assign them seats. These pawns provide opportunities for projective techniques; they make good scapegoats themselves, and serve as a safety valve. As for their mythical behavior problems—you and the class can have a field day discussing and correcting them.

COURTESY

You think your class is "rude and scant of courtesy"? Just a trifle short of the gentle virtues? In fact they aren't even civil, much less polite? Take heart, teacher; this can be one of the nicest challenges of your year. Polished manners result from a delicate sensitivity to the feelings of others, combined with daily practice, and you know how important they are for the children's present and future happiness and success. Well worth some school time. Your part, Mrs. Post, is merely to set a tone; then set a few goals and sit back. Enjoy watching them teach each other.

And to set the tone, all you must do is extend to one and all a courtesy fit for kings. Earned or unearned. Everyone gets your royal treatment in respect and courtesy. Please don't wait for disrespectful problem kids to respect you first, because Hades will freeze over and melt before this happens. Ordinarily, if they had known real respect in their backgrounds, they wouldn't be problem kids; you know that. As you take the initiative and show them marked respect, you will keep better control of the atmosphere, and eventually you'll reap a few rewards, a few tokens.

Now, at times of extreme provocation, you can direct embarrassment away from yourself by saying, "Is that the best you can do?" Or, "Is that your best thinking?" In some neighborhoods you could appeal to the respect due the office of teacher.

In schools where excellence permeated the eager air, I questioned teachers on this subject of teaching courtesy. Here are some of their suggestions.

Credit card–courtesy of . . . .

No! Courtesy Credit Card. Print COURTESY cards, with a surprise privilege on back of each. An especially considerate child may take a card–the top card. No peeking in stack. Examples of rewards: Extra drink of water . . . . First choice in music free sing . . . . Extra time in resource center.

. . . . "the very pink of courtesy"

Once a month have a room Politeness Day. Each student makes and decorates a construction paper button which reads "I'M POLITE." This day, any impolite action in the classroom invites corrective action. An offending student is asked to remove his badge, and any class member who sees the rudeness has authority to make the request. In halls, or in other rooms, rudeness is merely noted and reported when the group returns to homeroom. At 3:15 all who are still wearing buttons get extra points on their citizenship grades.

Courtesy contest

Make a class list on graph paper. Outstanding acts of courtesy score points. Children fill in squares themselves. Caution: Monitor this carefully. It's easy for the tempted to chisel a little.

Revolt against ruffians

Ask insolent child to write on good manners as an asset. This essay *shouldn't be a confessional;* instead, it should be impersonal. Require him to read it to the class.

NOTE-WRITING

Note-writing brings its greatest detrimental influence to the writer himself, for it diverts thinking from a task at hand and concerns itself with trivia–even from child's viewpoint. Your policy as teacher is to adroitly discourage note-writing rather than punish it.

English–from theory to practical

Intercept a note. Grade it for punctuation, spelling, capitalization. Use the grade for writer's language arts mark for the day. An additional comment at bottom of page about direct objects, verb aggreement, subjunctive, can be marvelously tongue in cheek.

The third man

Intercept a note. Orally ask the questions which the note asks. For instance, Susie has written to Mary, "Will you meet me after school?" Ask Mary, "Will you meet Susie after school?" If she says "yes," then tell Mary, "The answer is 'yes'." At this point you'll have the class with you. Your next remark can well be a short comment on how easy it would be to take care of such matters at recess or passing.

Latest press release

Intercept a note. Read it. If it doesn't seriously embarrass, post it on bulletin board.

Fundamentals only, my good fellow

When a student is note-writing rather than note-taking, glance over his shoulder and say softly but abruptly, "I disagree." Follow this opener with something light-hearted and irrelevant, such as:

"Yugoslav peasants do not need another shipload of old Wall Street Journals." Usually, no more hint is needed: the student gets back to work.

Underground communication

Intercept a note and after starting with the student's salutation and perhaps the writer's first sentence, switch from the text to a foolish jingle, something like–

Diddle, diddle, dumpling
My son John
Went to bed with his britches on
One shoe off and the other shoe on
Diddle, diddle dumpling
My son John.

I can assure you the class will gasp as you start reading the first sentence of the note.

Stamped CENSORED

If note's contents are unsavory, casually remark, "Maybe next time I'll read not only the salutation and a jingle, but our local author's work as well." Class will gasp even though they don't know contents of note.

CONCLUSION

Man has numerous ways of communicating, but many teachers are convinced students have mastered only one, talking. A curious corollary, but worth noting, is the fact that teachers tend to be among the most talkative of adults. So, if you're an environmentalist, you know how you would tackle that problem.

To gather all your radiant beams of joy into a fused, lustrous class, you must have their attention–at least from time to time. Adults might respond most readily to a variety of charming, clever comments; children, however, also welcome a pre-arranged sound or action signal. They're comfortable with a touch of ceremony, a bit of tradition unique to Room 103.

Pesky problems such as tattling, swearing, lack of courtesy, can be pleasantly alleviated or dissolved through remedial teaching steps.

The frequency of clowning, horsing around or constant chattering thrusts a new importance on erasing them. Are they symptomatic of something? Certainly. Serious symptions? Sometimes, and sometimes not. But totaled, these incidents have greater impact than the sum of the components, for your actions in settling these affairs directly contribute to the room's tone. This is the ripple result. And a dozen or two little incidents can be as wearing on you as a major crisis. That's the exhausted-teacher result.

When correcting a child's actions and speech, you won't necessarily muffle or damage his individuality. You'll enhance it, if you do your job well. Individuality is expressed in a deeply independent spirit. A person can be a conformist and still be very much an individual, providing he retains his spunkiness and conforms from conviction, never from fear. As easily as he can step into and out of a pair of shoes, a truly strong individual can step into and out of conformity with the customs of the group and the fashion of the hour. By the same token, an eccentric may indeed be a real independent–or he may be a fraud, incapable of authentic individual thinking and action.

Most of us will agree that the spirited child's spirit is precious and must be preserved.

Concerning misdeeds our aim is to teach the child the language of reason, of cause and effect; but we're talking to an individual who best understands the language of action, for he lives in an action world. Any diplomat worthy of his profession would converse, at least in part, in the language which his guest prefers. So, in dealing with children, a discerning but brief talk combined with a simple action requirement will bring better results than either talk or action alone.

. . . . . A time for silence

Several constructive exercises for children who keep on talking to their own detriment and in spite of repeated warnings:

1. Have the child write a paragraph on what would happen if he were a jet pilot and kept on talking while the control tower was giving him instructions.
2. If the class were to be filmed on TV during school hours, ask a talkative youngster to describe how he would conduct himself. How would he most impress his audience?
3. Ask him to describe, on paper or on tape, some of the things which might have happened to the astronauts if they had

been busy mouthing snide remarks to one another on one of their voyages.

4. Ask him to find out and report back to you on what happens to ball players when they talk too much or get cheeky.

9 Combat--Conduct and Nuisance Problems

There once lived a scholarly, cosmopolitan fellow by the name of Erasmus (1467-1536) who liked to think. He thought. For a cloistered gentleman of the Renaissance he came to some surprising conclusions.

He believed in universal education–rich and poor, men and women–the only limit would be the individual's ability. The next surprise: he advised the use of stories, games, pictures and objects as good teaching method–and that was almost five centuries ago. He expressed little patience with grammar teachers who wasted precious years hammering rules of grammar into children. Since he believed in appealing to interest, it's not surprising that he felt "teaching by beating is not a liberal education, and the school master should not indulge in too strong and too frequent language of blame." Strange, isn't it, that appealing to children's natural interests is still considered a modern and dewy-fresh idea?

In this chapter we'll consider something of a blend of typical physical behavior problems: squirming, out of seats, stealing, fighting, throwing things and gum-chewing. Ordinarily, youngsters are well aware that teachers should not be indulging toward students, and we may quite properly ask them, courteously, why they should be an exception to the general rule. As always, the teacher's tone and attitude are vital. So is her promptness.

Squirming often stems from physical discomfort or mild fatigue, and thus a change of pace brings welcomed relief. If you notice a consistent restlessness, you may want to provide the children with valid excuses for getting out of their seats–paper, writing at board, library corner. Having the group stand in a circle for art or science demonstrations is good. Later in this chapter you'll find distinctive measures.

Possessions such as weapons and toys are often best handled by pleasantly enforcing the impersonal rules of room and school.

Closely related to this topic is stealing, and the interviewed teachers offered an abundance of ideas on how they have handled various situations. Most teachers don't encounter this problem as often as one might expect, but usually they place great importance on dealing with it thoughtfully and considerately.

Then we'll touch on fighting, how it varies from neighborhood to neighborhood, and we'll offer some guidelines to help teachers develop their own ways of dealing with this difficulty.

Flying objects, except for paper airplanes, are almost nonexistent in some schools and quite a nuisance in others. Misbehaving with them seems to be contagious.

More needless sharp verbal scuffles are fought over old fashioned gum-chewing than over any other single school rule—and it's the easiest action of all to handle in a tactful or surprising way.

RESTLESS SQUIRMING AND RESISTENCE

When a class becomes squirmy and a little inattentive, kindness requires that a teacher do something to relieve the situation. Lots of time teachers whose classes are well under control may say simply, "Take a short break." However, many circumstances can prohibit this freedom: the group doesn't yet know how to set its own limits, the principal disapproves of large numbers of students being out of their seats, or the teacher is not sure of herself or she fears a few scamps will start a melee.

Included here are a few suggestions which teachers offered to share, suggestions which they felt would make life easier for other teachers and students on those squirmy days.

Dress rehearsal for a fire drill

Announce a little ahead of time a practice fire drill for room 103, say for 2:00 pm. Then at 2:00 have the class line up, turn off lights, close doors, whatever your fire rules include. With no buzzer sounding, the children tend to be less excited. March the children to your fire drill exit. Stop. Turn around. Return to the classroom. You understand your principal well enough to know whether you should mention this expedition to him ahead of time.

7th inning stretch

Call it. You may want to explain to your class about this custom—or maybe let one of your boys tell them. Let the class stand at their desks and wiggle for a few minutes.

Around the world

This learning game makes a good ten minute break. It can be played with math or vowel cards. Many times children will elect to play it during indoor recess.
Directions: Give a child some arithmetic flash cards. He shows one to the first child. If she answers incorrectly, she remains seated. If she answers correctly, she takes the pack and shows a card to the child sitting behind her. The pack changes hands with each correct answer. Continue around the room.

Sit your hands still

This device is good for those times when the whole class is restless and you're not going to try to keep them still, yet you do need their undivided attention for a few minutes. Children usually sit still when their hands are not moving. Please don't just ask pupils to fold their hands on top of their desks. Instead, 1) ask them to place their hands on top of their heads; 2) ask them to sit on their hands; 3) ask them to hold their own wrists; 4) ask them to take one hand and hold the other wrist and with their second hand touch their nose, etc. If not done too frequently, children will have lots of fun following these requests.

Drop it on them

In sign language teach a whole lesson. The project is a wonderful lesson in the art of communication without speech, and it should make children more alert to the many ways we convey thoughts. It's a big help in retaining the youngster who tunes the teacher's words out. The first time a teacher tries this approach, it comes as a shock to the class. It can be repeated often, as often as once a week, and it doesn't grow stale. Demonstrations in science can be adapted to this technique.

Good example: A 15-minute penmanship exercise in sign language. Have your supplies ready ahead of time or get them ready without commenting to class. Tell one child by pointing and signs to pass booklets. Tell another by signs to pass paper. Tell pupils to take their pencils out. Put right and wrong examples on the board . . . and all the time, never a word. If a child asks a question, put your finger to your lips and shake your head.

Several teachers told me that the children most likely to resist directions are the ones who are allowed to do exactly as they please at home. Naturally, if after a few tries, the case persists, the mother should be advised about how much easier she could make her child's experience if she would lessen her unusual permissiveness. Here are steps some teachers take when faced with this.

"I won't move"

Help the child. Go behind him and lift firmly by his armpits while you put your knee behind him; lift and boost into the place where he should be. Then say, "There, that's fine." Of course, do this without anger but with assurance. Primary only.

Either . . . or

Offer him a choice. "Either come with the class or sit on the floor back of my desk." This gives him a degree of freedom by letting him make the choice. Also, extend an open invitation to him to rejoin the group anytime he feels willing to do as they are doing.

Author's note: Personally, I never like to ask a child to sit on the floor as part of a punishment, although many fine teachers do. I feel that, at those moments when we're stressing more grown-up behavior requirements, or more self-respect, we should do our part by extending the grown-up courtesy of a chair, or at least a cushion.

Now this leads us into the related problem–the child who refuses to sit in his seat. Lots of times this is just a bad habit. You might try these corrections a few times and then, if the habit isn't broken, you'd better delve deeper into the whole matter.

Seats are made for . . . . looking at

Don't bother asking him one more time about sitting. Have him stand next to his desk until lesson's end. During recitations this isn't so bad, but when others start to read or write, it's awkward. Usually, just once is all you have to do this.

All eyes on me

If a child keeps falling or getting out of his seat, take the chair away from him for a while. Make him sit on the floor at his desk. In about ten minutes ask him if he has learned his lesson.

Fasten your seat belt

In a friendly voice tell him that today he can pretend he's a pilot, and the first thing pilots do when they sit down in the cockpit is fasten their seat belts. Leash the little "enfant terrible" to his seat. In some classes youngsters like this device so well that it has to be made unattractive by adding to it the denial of another privilege. Otherwise you may have a rash of little boys leaving their seats in order to be punished. If you teach in one of those schools where you just don't send students to the office, this technique–done in a very friendly way–is good with extreme cases.

WEAPONS AND TOYS

Evidently, children very quickly learn to follow rules when their treasures are in jeopardy, for the interviewed teachers did not offer much new material on this subject.

One school, which has a diverse student body, has about eliminated this problem. The all-school rules state that there will be no toys, squirt guns, Boy Scout knives, etc., in the building. The first violation brings a warning from the classroom teacher; and on the second violation the child is sent to the office. There the principal speaks to him and a letter is sent home.

With rubber bands . . . who needs toys?

David brought a bounteous supply of rubber bands to school, and equipped his friends with all they thought they needed. Later, when the teacher discovered the ring leader, he was required to bring a chair to the wastebasket in the front of the room. Then he was asked to cut each rubber band in his possession into three pieces. While he was snipping, everyone who had received part of his largess was invited to step forward and "let" David cut those bands, too. Needless to say, this was a great opportunity. Everyone in the room who had any sort of rubber band brought it up in a spirit of quiet glee. The more our friend David complained, the more his buddies scoured their desks for a few more bands.

Obviously, if a child brought an undue supply of tacks or pins to school, you would find it easy to develop an alternate similar procedure.

STEALING

"Who steals my purse, steals trash . . . " And if it's all the same to you, we'll have that trash back, thank you! Since your students have heard numerous parental admonitions about stealing property, why not give your remedial talk a little different slant when you have an incident? First, you might mention stealing in good fun—as in a ball game. Or, with older children, perhaps comment on "midnight requisitions" (people in schools and offices taking supplies for legitimate purposes without filling out proper forms). Then ease into the discussion of indirect stealing, such as slander or wasting an employer's time. If the discussion has been brief enough to keep everyone's interest, it should deepen the children's sense of right. From merely refraining from swiping, he learns respect for our moral obligations to others.

Over and over, the excellent teachers I interviewed mentioned the importance of building an atmosphere of trust. They advise, "Expect honesty." A surprising number felt free to leave their handbags out and never had any trouble. Those who found it necessary to lock things did so very quietly, almost without negative comment. They all wanted to trust.

As I talked with them, they offered to share these many kind and imaginative suggestions. I hope these will be of help to you should you need guidance.

29 plus 1 equals 30 letters

Some rare old English coins were passed around the room. One disappeared. Angrily, the teacher announced that the whole class must stay after school until the missing coin reappeared. At 3:35 she was perched on a swaying limb; the culprit had not summoned the nerve to announce his guilt publicly; mothers would be worrying.

The teacher explained to the class that she couldn't keep them any longer, although she knew it wasn't fair to let the guilty go scot free. Yet she was sure he was very sorry for his actions. Were there any suggestions?

One girl offered this idea. Have each student write a note. Each innocent child would say, "I did not take it" and sign. The guilty one was to say, "I did take it and I'm sorry" and sign. The teacher's part in the pact was to let the offender remain anonymous that day, and to settle with him later. It worked like a charm.

Within these walls

Dues of 5¢ a week are appropriate if you have a room treasury. Then if a book-clip, a good pen or some such item disappears within the room, have the class treasurer buy a replacement out of the funds. One can really see how this would promote a sense of group responsibility.

Suspect assigned the role of Sherlock

Brian, a boy with a good record, took a paint box from the room and was caught redhanded on the playground. He insisted another boy had given him the box.

The teacher wrote a note and had Brian take it to every room; the note asked other teachers to check their paint supplies. On his round, Brian was to look over the boys to see if he could locate the donor of the paints. Since Brian was a sensitive boy who would feel pangs of regret, the homeroom teacher didn't try to get him to confess, for she felt just carrying the note was enough. Later on, he did confess of his own accord.

Trust you? Of course I do

After you have corrected a stealing incident, take an early opportunity to show the child you trust him. Have him carry money in an envelope to the office–ask him to get your purse in the back room–ask him to lock the desk drawer.

Temptation no longer twinkles

School property is for all to enjoy and use wisely. Early inform children that any portable object in the room may be checked out for a week-end. Here's the reason: Often, children are momentarily enticed into stealing something, but by the time they get it home they have lost interest in it. At this point the child has a problem; there's danger in trying to return the thing stolen, and the safest course is to put it in a waste can in some alley. This dilemma is eliminated by the check-out system. When that is operating, many times parents will call the school because Johnny has brought home something from the classroom, but after they've been reassured, they are much impressed with the school system.

No tickee–no washee

No marker–No graded papers. Occasionally colored pencils or felt markers will disappear from a teacher's desk. You might try, "I'm sorry, but I can't mark any papers until I find my marking pen." Almost invariably a child will find it, usually before the end of the day. Wisdom suggests that the teacher avoid questioning or scolding.

When in doubt . . . try trusting

A purse has disappeared. Tell children you're sure the thief must regret yielding to temptation; if this purse is returned within 24 hours, you'll not investigate further. Choose a deposit receptacle into which the thief is to slip the purse. Nearly always it will be returned. Afterwards, let the class talk about the long-range benefits of honesty, taking special care not to cast any innuendoes.

Dissolving the denial

If a child fibs about a stolen item, write a letter or phone the home. Ask parent, "Does Dave have a blue pen?" If the parent says No, then ask, "May I have your permission to talk to Dave about this?" Rarely is it denied. When you do talk to the child, be gentle, and be careful in what you say. Please give him an opportunity to save face.

If he cares, show him you care

When a youngster is sensitive to law, and has been caught stealing, even getting caught is a punishment. The balance can be mild and still be effective. Perhaps returning the merchandise is enough.

If he doesn't care, show him you care

When a worldly youngster, indifferent to law has been caught stealing, he views getting caught as merely an occupational hazard, not as a punishment. Your hope is to have him feel reasonable regret. You can have him write an essay; or it may seem right to involve one of his parents.

"I'm sorry" plus "let's be friends"

Gary highly valued his set of Presidential statues. Billy stole them. Later Billy returned them, apologized, and felt so badly about his actions that he voluntarily offered to make a special present for Gary. In later years this teacher has handled many cases of stealing along the same lines: restitution, apology, and an extra act of friendliness on the thief's part. If there is no initial hostility in the thief's thought, he's glad to do something to show he really meant it when he said, "I'm sorry."

Information wanted–no reward

Pass out plain paper. Instruct children to print, not write, any information they happen to know about the theft. Explain they are not tattling; they are doing the thief a favor, since you're almost sure to catch the culprit later, and things will go much tougher for him then. Reassure the class that there will be no scene; you'll speak with the thief in private. Almost always, someone in the room saw the act or the missing article, or has learned confidential information.

Protection racket

Lead the class in a general discussion about the fallacy of buying friendship. Strengthen the youngsters who could be imposed on by asking them to come to you and you'll protect their identity. Add, as an example, that there isn't a mother of any child in the room who would give money to one of her friends or acquaintances who demanded it. Explain that blackmail is evil. Giving in to it supports it, rewards it, strengthens it.

There's nothing here I wouldn't give you

One teacher has been making an offer for years, and no one has ever taken her up on it. She tells her students she doesn't want to see them tempted. If there's anything in the room they want so much they might be tempted to take it, let her know; she'll give it to them. She doesn't have any stealing either.

FIGHTING

In the children's minds, puppy-dog wrestling and pummeling your buddy are not fighting. After all, "The other fellow was having fun too." Surface scrappiness doesn't always mean that a child is swimming in hostility. Sometimes it's mere habit. Often it reflects home standards, for many working-class parents teach their boys to fight, and are proud of a youngster who "can lick every kid on the block."

As many teachers know only too well, physical force is a dominant fact of life in some poorer areas. This is a main reason why Blacks tend to play rougher; it's not because they're rougher by nature; they're not. But even fun-fighting can become serious. Then it degenerates into personalities and bitterness.

Any schoolyard referee must first raise thought from personalities to principles–rules of fairness, consideration. In supervising playing youngsters there's a big difference between realistic caring and anxious caution. Caring for either people or things stems from an attitude of appreciation for their worth. Acting from excessive caution means acting from a base of fear. Carefulness and caution are words whose paths diverge only slightly in the beginning, but the angle is set.

One very gentle and effective teacher told me that when she has real fights to settle, she always ask the youngster after he's calmed down, "Whatever it is, is it worth fighting for?" She maintains a rule in her classroom that any child who is stealing, fighting, lying or name-calling is not ready for school, and is better off at home. Then she phones the home and sends the youngster there at the next natural break. May I add that her class enrollment consists of children from every conceivable background?

City or suburb, often you can prevent more fights through a chat with parents than by any other step. Casually and tactfully try directing their attention to the fact that most "middle class" parents teach children to avoid most fights. If you've been subtle, they won't answer you directly, but they'll happily adopt the hint. You'll know it, because their offspring's skirmishes will drop in number, often dramatically.

Coping with a little warrior himself is another story. If he's finding that others pick on him frequently, he has probably asked for it, consciously or unconsciously. He might need an explanation of how every person tends to attract his own thinking. Sometimes, too, he's got a reputation to live down before he can have peace. Thus, he may not have swarms of friends immediately upon turning over a new leaf, but he won't have to battle his way through life; fighting is but one way to resolve a matter. In conclusion you might suggest to him, "Don't give up your right to decide for yourself which way a difference is going to be settled."

Bullying is a special kind of fighting. Every bully has had his life warped in some way. And, for the record, nagging is an adult form of bullying, or so I am told.

In talking things over with a bully fighter, a three-way conversation with parent, child and teacher is suggested. Make the child face what he's done. Let him state his position–this weakens his defensiveness. Let him explain why he's done nothing wrong if he's still thinking this way. Extreme cases are sometimes corrected or alleviated by letting or making a child transfer to another school.

Any mental atmosphere is contagious, and aggression can become highly contagious.

Excellent comments and suggestions came abundantly when I questioned teachers about handling fighting. Here are a few of them for your consideration.

Lock the barn door ahead of time

Stage a mock fight with role-playing. Structure an incident of fighting. Ask about eight children to participate. Select a pair to scuffle. The others are by-standers. Afterwards, have a group discussion on the causes of fighting and the different kinds of fights: with fists, words, nasty looks, etc. Suggest available alternatives to fighting, if the class doesn't offer these points naturally. These alternatives may be included:

1. Tell offender to cut it out.
2. Tell teacher or playground supervisor.
3. Walk away from impending fights–this takes a strong person.

One needle and a long thread

If a child rips the clothes of another, have him repair the damage with needle and thread. Naturally, it won't be a satisfactory job, but it will help him learn to take more responsibility for his actions. He'll remember the task.

Well, mom, it was like this

You have a scrappy youngster who has not responded to warnings. Stop his next fight. As soon as convenient take him to the office and dial his home. When his mother answers, explain to her the boy has been in another fracas. Now you'll let him tell her the whole story. You stand next to him as he talks. This way, parents get a very straight story. Also it gives the mother time, before her son arrives home, to think over how she wants to handle the incident.

We stick together, ugh

In severe cases of fighting make the two children involved do everything together for two days or so–until they become very tired of each other's company.

A playground–not a fight arena

You have a scrappy child who is ruining the playground for others. Deny him the privilege of using it. Specify exact number of days and whether before and/or after school. This requires follow-through on your part. 1) You'll need to inform the home. 2) You or another adult must be outside during quoted hours. If it's a morning denial, send the child inside as soon as he arrives, and give him work to do. If it's an afternoon restriction, someone must see that the child goes directly home.

Not even a bully can fight by himself

When you dismiss the class, leave the bully in the room while you walk youngsters to the dismissal door. By the time you return two minutes will have elapsed. This is long enough for a child in an empty classroom, and he'll have felt the separation. Let him go with only a brief remark, not a scolding.

I'd like to have you meet

If there has been a fight which you are quite sure was unprovoked by the loser, have the bully winner meet the loser's parents for a conference. This gets through a tough shell. Generally speaking, clear this conference with your principal ahead of time–you may even pick up additional support from him.

Visiting hours are . . . .

If there has been a fight and one youngster's injuries are serious enough to hospitalize him, take the winner to the room and let him see for himself the results.

In this corner we have

Separate fighting children. Speak firmly and briefly. Let the sureness of your voice inform them that there is definite outside control. At the moment don't reason with them about their fighting. In a few minutes you'll notice changed expressions, and feelings will have calmed. Now talk to each child separately. In a warm voice explain your earlier abruptness and tell them you'd always rather talk and reason with students.

FLYING OBJECTS

Most children love to test their throwing agility for the same deep-rooted reason they like to wiggle their toes in wet sand. It feels good. The pleasure of communicating by hitting someone with a flying object (yet with no intention to hurt) is hard for a child to give up once he has discovered it.

Discovery and creativity. Which came first? Rather come and go together, don't they? Connecting these present-day clarion calls of education with the perennial childish aptitude for paper airplanes and paper wads, we see their captivating challenge.

Seeing's one thing, acting's another. We teach art to children. We teach them gym. Yet when they combine art talents, and communicate non-verbally by means of Identified Flying Objects, we exclaim, "This will never do!" True a child in a classroom mustn't interrupt others, and certainly we must "gently correct and weed out bad Inclinations and settle in him good Habits." (John Locke) But what of "the captivating challenge"?

Almost any teacher who has taught in both city and suburbs has noticed that in the suburbs there are more paper airplanes of various sorts, and spit balls are quite rare; whereas the ratio goes the other way in industrial neighborhoods. When I go back into the city to teach, and if I find myself confronted with the problem of paper wads and spit balls, I believe I will take time and teach those children how to make all sorts of airplanes.

When interviewing teachers on paper wads and airplanes, I received mostly routine answers–with a few exceptions. I was much impressed with those few. These teachers offered to share their experiences in the hope of helping readers of this book. That's my hope, too.

Plain airplanes? passe!

If you have a number of children folding these deuced little annoyances, here's an excellent correction. Plan a special art lesson on creative folding of paper. Then, if after all this imaginative folding, you still have a few old-style airplanes sailing around, invite a small group of children in for an after-school session of paper folding.

The natives have their own art forms

Paper airplanes were a real nuisance in one school. The teachers tried an airplane unit-in-study, but it didn't help. Then they became more radical. A book on folding paper airplanes was brought into the classrooms, and everyone was asked to make folded planes–the fancier the folding, the better. The next move was to have every child fly these creations each morning for five minutes, and then the planes were put away in cupboard or desks. These practice sessions lasted for about three weeks and were leading up to a grand finale, a contest on the playground one sunny morning. After this, the children were glad to forget them.

Bull's eye Benny

Invite your paper wad expert or your spit-ball-maker par excellence to return after school. When he arrives, have his workshop ready. It'll consist of a desk with an impressively thick pile of manilla paper on it and a waste basket placed at exactly the right challenging distance. Then direct him to set down and start making more paper wads (or spit balls); each one is to be shot into the basket. At first this is fun. As he continues, he's increasingly aware that the fun is on his own time and his mouth may be getting dry. All the while he's not to leave his seat for any reason. Soon he'll start eyeing the remaining stack of paper. This is your cue to think about letting him go home.

Unidentified flying objects . . . identified

Eraser- and chalk-throwing had become a problem for several days, and the teacher had caught only two pupils red-handed. The next morning she made it a point to arrive in the room before the youngsters. While the room was still clean, she named these two boys as sole members of a committee responsible for the entire room. They were to pick up every chalk and paper fragment before they could leave for their next class.

They complained bitterly about the unfairness of this world in general and this teacher in particular. She told them that if they couldn't persuade classmates not to throw objects, the committee-men were to report the unruly students. Also she added that, though it wasn't completely fair, many times on this planet a few suffer for the sins of many.

GUM CHEWING

The chicle tree is native to the semi-tropical regions of South and Central America. Have you ever seen one of those plantations? The owners are amazingly wealthy men, but that fact won't surprise any school teacher.

Gum chewing isn't serious, but if there's an all-school rule against it, or if gum chewing gets on your nerves, there are many good-natured ways of getting children willingly to co-operate. Here's a nice selection of suggestions; hopefully you'll find one to fit your personality.

If I have five pices of gum

One teacher, tired of mentioning the all-school no-gum-chewing rule, took action. Just before class she stuffed five sticks of gum in her mouth. During class she chewed and chewed. At the same time she presented a new concept in math–orally. Lots of snickering among the students, but never again was gum-chewing a problem with the group.

". . . to each according to his needs"

If you have a student chewing gum, insist he give you two pieces. If he gives you an argument, tell him you *need* two pieces because your mouth is twice as large as his.

Before entering this sanctuary

Just before the bell, stand at the door. As the students enter hand out small pieces of paper, saying only, "For your gum." Quietly courteous, this method eliminates time-consuming, spotlight processions to the wastebaskets.

A variation: Walk down the aisles and hand out papers for gum deposit to seated students.

Where there's gum, there's wrappers

Gum-chewing is rampant. Have class give up their recess one morning. After the others have come in take your class out and let them pick up candy and gum wrappers in the yard.

Gum-chewing day

One affairs-of-state decision for room 103, which can be resolved early in the year, is gum-chewing day, a weekly occurrence. The group elects the specific day, and definite rules are determined. One rule is: Any student leaving for messenger duty, library, or gym must throw out his gum before he leaves the classroom.

Bubble bubble, double trouble

Bubble gum chewing costs at school. Fine the child 5¢ and put it into the class kitty. If the child doesn't have 5¢, keep the whole class after school until someone lends him hard cash. Fines exacted can be used toward a party.

Gummy gala

Once a month plan a gum-chewing party which lasts about 30 minutes each time. At the party everyone in the room must chew gum and join in the games. The highlight is a contest and the pupil who makes the biggest bubble wins a foolish prize. At the end of the party pass the waste basket, and everyone throws his gum in it. The moral: there's a time and place for everything.

Someone put that gum under there

First offense brings a warning. Second offense brings a session after school. The student must remain and scrape the old gum from the bottom of each desk and seat. You provide an old silver knife and the Kleenex. In theory the third offense brings a stint on a block of auditorium seats. This approach of handling gum chewing was developed in a 6th grade discussion several years ago. Since its inception, the teacher has never had to resort to step three.

CONCLUSION

In this chapter we have discussed behavior problems which, essentially, involve physical movement. There were suggestions for correcting squirming when it comes from fatigue. One suggestion, the sign language lesson, was offered as a corrective to boredom squirms. Then we considered that peculiar, but still normal, resistence which finds expression in unwillingness to sit in chairs.

Effectively handling the weapon and toy problem, by setting up and enforcing a uniform, all-school rule, was cited. The interviewed teachers offered quite a variety of ways of handling stealing, but without exception they considered trust the dominant quality to nurture in the classroom atmosphere. Also brought out: stealing is not always of physical objects.

Next we moved on to considering fighting among students, and why it is more prevalent in poorer neighborhoods–at least, a few reasons it's more prevalent there. I'm most grateful for the nummerous suggestions teacher offered for settling and ending fighting.

A penchant for paper airplanes among students can give the teacher a wonderful opener for leading children to use their creative talents–even to team contests. Included was a suggestion for dealing with your local paper wad king.

Instead of gaggle over chewing gum, some teachers have a party. Interviewees offered enough ideas on handling gum-chewing politely and quietly that getting annoyed over gum seems quite pointless.

You know, it's over these little concerns such as pencil sharpening or gum chewing, day to day things, that most pupils make up their minds about a teacher's instinctive fairness and courtesy. They don't try to judge her on the far out cases. Maybe we shouldn't, either.

10 Work and Study Habits

A motivated student is a girl or a boy with a purpose. Simply stated, purpose means being concerned about accomplishing something. An individual's purpose is developed only as he becomes aware of new values which promise to make life richer than it was with the values he previously held.

Many poor students have little interest in anything beyond the basics of life. In this state they are bored and boring people. As a trained teacher you already know the power of friendly, understanding talks. In addition you can ask them to bring in three or four newspaper clippings which they find appealing . . . . these might give you a few acceptable clues for an approach. Sometimes an interest inventory (see page 24) will spotlight latest possibilities.

Some poor students use indifference as protective coloring to hide fears of failure. Honest praise of a specific piece of their work, a specific talent, or a specific character trait does wonders. Praise them in front of their friends. Some mediocre students are apathetic because they carry the oppressive burden of false conviction that they "just don't have it" in any department of school.

In our concern for helping poor students become better students—indeed, good students—let's consider the qualities necessary for a good student.

1. *Perception*—of what can be discerned by the senses, including the subtle, small, or apparently insignificant.

As you think about this, you'll realize there are also nonacademic ways in which a student can work on this trait. Sharpness of attention to nuances adds grace to social life, touch to playing or singing music, and finesse to acting.

2. *Reason*—To calculate, to think, the power of comprehending, especially in orderly, rational ways.

You can help students marshal facts, look for patterns, and slot items into major and minor categories without ever mentioning you're helping them learn to reason.

3. *Memory*—The power of recall.

A most important ingredient of a good memory is interest in the information. We know from experience that we forget those things which mean little or nothing to us.

4. *Application*—The act of putting information to use.

A most important factor here is an inclination to give close attention.

5. *Judgment*—The process of, or skill in, forming an opinion, or evaluating, by discerning or comparing.

This is one of the ultimate goals of real education.

Now let's move on to the immediate application of daily details. None of the next points is terribly important in itself, but in the aggregate they make a tremendous difference in the way the final score reads. Combined, they bring greater habits of order, coherence and completeness, attributes which contribute toward success in any department of life.

Although not an end in itself, order is a tool which will serve the child well. Start building for order and coherence with larger factors: complete room supplies, moderately neat desks (of both teacher and pupil), and organized notebooks. Making a child redo a paper because it has botches on it, when his desk and notebook are in a colossal, chronic chaos, is much like trying to put a silk dress on a goat. Ideally, you should work at teaching the child a reasonably systematic desk procedure first, but many times you just can't. Your next choice is to work on both aspects simultaneously, but there are times when you can't do that either. In some cases work on teaching him to improve his papers, while yourself never forgetting that an easy order promotes growth, and our ultimate goal is success, not order.

DIRECTION-FOLLOWING

Learning to follow instructions accurately is the easiest way for a student to add to his success painlessly. Teachers like his sincere effort. Always, they feel, he's "trying" even when he isn't expending much energy. Sometimes we need to reassure a student that he's not compromising his individuality by following instructions—individuality and non-conformity are definitely not interchangeable terms. Occasionally a student ignores or disobeys petty directions as a device for defying the adult world. If we find this widespread in our classroom, we are wise to re-examine the tone and wording of our directions. However, if it's an isolated case, try telling such a youngster, "It's just as easy to conform on inconsequential things as to non-conform. Save your non-conforming energies for matters which count."

Another task for a willfully balky student: tell him how many of his fellow students have raised test and IQ scores over brighter friends by carefully following directions; he's going to leave himself behind needlessly. And he's not going to help nor hurt anyone but himself.

If you sense a deeper rebelliousness, or a touch of personal antagonism, you may want to remind him of the minutiaeladen directions which you must follow in your job. This gets to them. The fact that a teacher must follow someone's orders pleases them. Resistence melts.

When you give directions, start with a clear statement of goal. Then follow with a general route or method, and then give specific details. If the class is doing poorly, ask yourself: Am I concise? Do I keep it simple? For every teacher who fails to give adequate instructions, there must be 50 who just talk too much.

Certainly, intensified direction-following practice improves student skill. These are good for the times when the class needs a five minute pace change or break. Here are some suggestions which teachers offered to share.

. . . . and the next voice

Turn on a tape recorder. Give explicit directions for a lesson. Ask one or two children to repeat. Have class listen to tape.

With duly impressive ceremony

Use workbook pages for practice in improving direction-following abilities of a class. If you do this four or five times before an important, standardized test, the children will be much more comfortable on the big day. This kind of exercise pulls the class into a feeling of oneness, which the children love.

Make it an occasion. 1) Clear desk tops. 2) Separate desks. 3) Two pencils on each desk. 4) No talking. 5) Set timer. 6) Read directions aloud. 7) Release timer and Go! Without the pressure of a for-real test, children enjoy a click, click, click atmosphere, and it is for only 30 to 45 minutes, or less.

Let me think, what did she say?

Each child develops a written set of three, four, or five step directions. Example: 1) Go to globe and point to Africa. 2) Write your name backwards on board. 3) Give a pencil to the teacher. Jane calls on Peter and orally gives him her directions *once.* If Peter completes the task without stumbling, he reads his directions and calls on Chris. Whenever a student makes a mistake, teacher chooses the next candidate, thus assuring that those most in need of this drill will receive practice.

Good listeners' club

Everybody belongs in this club. Officers are a president, a vice-president and a secretary. The club roster has a ditto sheet picture of each member, which the member has colored in crayons to look like himself. Faces, cut out, are placed on a bulletin board with pins. If a student errs in not listening while another is talking, refuses to follow directions, or talks while another is talking–one of the club's officers removes the offender's picture and gives it back to him for the rest of the day. Just before dismissal a club officer gathers all faces from the desks and displays them again. Visiting teachers find this a big help in maintaining a good tempo while they are teaching special lessons.

Changing Subjects

You're sorry to interrupt busy children–sorrier than they realize. But you must. Tell them that a large part of school fun is doing things in groups.

Put your ear to the ground as your first step in promoting smoother transitions. Acquire a sensitivity to class tenor by being quiet and mentally listening. Eye your top average students. As they are completing a lesson, announce a few more minutes for everyone.

Another helpful step is to ask your paper passers to distribute the next lesson's paper a few minutes prior to agenda time, but don't interrupt the children yourself until switching time. Some teachers have found a special hand or sound signal which proves to be a natural for their group. Splendid. Other teachers have smoothed transitions by using the stimulus of a variety of signals. Either way is fine, but ALWAYS stand when introducing the next subject.

Here are some of the techniques which a few thoughtful, sharp teachers use:

Names of the elect are

Write on board the names of children who are ready to proceed to the next subject or who otherwise followed directions. As you put names up, you will be asked, "Why are their names up there?" As others learn the reason, they hasten to comply.

Bittersweet, mauve, periwinkle blue

Children like direction signals which involve color. This approach also improves their listening attentiveness and helps to quiet the room.

Example: Ask children to take out a speller and two pencils as soon as you announce the word "violet." In full, firm voice start naming others colors, and gradually lower the tone of your voice. The room becomes hushed. When the noise level is at a good point, and their attention focused, call "violet."

Beethoven will do

Another older timer but very good. Play a few bars of a pleasing tune on the piano–same tune each time, of course.

Eins, zwei, drei . . . . funfzig

Teach your class to count to 50 in a foreign language. Even before they've mastered the task, you may use the numbers to time them. An example: You've asked everyone to put away his math book and take out his crayons. Give directions and start counting: children will count along with you, but they will also speed up. Counting in a foreign tongue makes a game. This technique can be used often; it doesn't wear out quickly.

Which side is winning?

Divide room into halves. Draw two boxes on board. During the day put ✓ marks in the section of the children who are ready first.

Prize? Winning team goes for drinks first, or leaves to get wraps first.

DAWDLING

Many children live in an enchanting land, a land where time stands still. Charmingly free from adult viewpoints, they love it. It makes it difficult, though, to impress them with our bells and schedules. Putting time to work for us is an important lesson. If it's deferred too long, the lesson becomes harder.

You have your work cut out for you, teacher. You're to teach the importance of living "now" and, in the same breath, the importance of preparing for the tomorrows. Focus on the word–perspective.

Just like adults, youngsters need goals and due dates. When the class is nibbling on their pencils and gazing at the walls, deadlines add sharpness which cuts into the apathy. Meeting a challenge within a specified time brings a feeling of accomplishment, self-respect and power over oneself.

Many background factors must be heeded but a huge part of the task is simply training youngsters into recognizing that clock hands move relentlessly. Here are some constructive suggestions teachers offered.

Gettin' started is mighty hard

Divide your slow poke's assignment into thirds. Ask him to let you know when he finishes the first portion–give him a star. For the second portion, another star. Naturally he'll get a third star when he completes the task.

Starting post to finishing line

On the bulletin board post correct finished work of the first ten students to complete a task. Post papers in order of completion.

Slaving away at nothing

A student sometimes looks as if he's working, but actually he's accomplishing nothing. Try persuasion first. Then stop at his desk and say, "I want to see you do five problems in the next three minutes." Later, stop at his desk, comment on completed problems, and say, "Now I want to see you do eight more problems in three minutes." Again, stop, comment on completed work, and add, "Please finish your paper in ten minutes and bring it to my desk."

Time stands still

Ask your dawdling friend to take his work to an ordinary table. Direct him to stand there and work until he finishes. It's uncomfortable to stand and write. He won't like it, but he will get busy and finish his work.

Time stands still throughout the land

A whole class is dragging. Use the biggest, noisiest test timer available. Place it on your desk. It dramatizes the coming event. Select a period of time, say 30 minutes. Ask each child to decide how much he will accomplish, and jot it down. His success is measured by how close he comes to his estimate. Results are remarkable in quantity and quality.

Hunger makes a faster worker

Have dawdler stay at noon and finish his work before he leaves for lunch. Stay with him. When he complains he's hungry, tell him you're hungry, too. If he goes home for lunch, be sure to check with his mother ahead of time, please.

It's no fun by yourself

When a dawdler becomes an idler and accomplishes almost nothing in a morning, send him home at noon to spend the rest of the day there. Tell him that by refusing to work, he has lost the privilege of coming to school. Don't use the word "suspend"—this makes him a hero in a negative way. Ask his mother to keep him in the house but not to punish him. You may think it wise to ask her to let him play with his toys but she is to avoid giving him companionship herself. Usually, she may let him go out and play at his normal arrival home time.

Poker chip Peter

Petie was a problem child with a very short interest-span. The teacher and the social worker decided on an incentive plan. Petie received a poker chip for every 20 minutes he worked hard. When he accumulated 20 chips, the two adults took him to lunch. At lunch they praised his progress and growth, and in reward for his growth they increadesd the time-span to 30 minutes. Again, when he had accumulated 20 chips, they took him to lunch. Once more, growth earned a time-span increase. So the pattern went until he reached the hour span. By this time he no longer needed help.

Either way she's going to kiss me

Sometimes children, especially little boys, can be teased into a degree of diligence. Tell them, "If you finish your work I'll kiss you. If you don't finish your work, I'll kiss you ten times." (For women teachers only!)

INCOMPLETE SUPPLIES

Children without proper supplies are rocks in the stream of group progress. No teacher needs to be told that they are a diverting influence to the task at hand.

Some homes are completely disorganized. It's not the children's fault they are without needed items. You must start tactfully—or not so tactfully—with their elders. Often a child could well have everything he needed if just one member of his family saw the importance.

As you think about it you'll realize that his is not a correctional problem so much as a growth-of-responsibility problem. A child must feel mild discomfort in his carefree disregard of his own interests. You can stretch him into accepting the day's demands on him.

Again, some suggestions by courtesy of practicing teachers who want very much to help these children.

Do Not Enter

Post a sign on the window of the classroom door. "Do not enter this room without a pencil and paper." Stick to it. (This is for upper grades only and for schools where neglect is widespread.)

Her name is now pawn shop Nellie

Perhaps, when you lend supplies, you rarely get them back. Ask student for a deposit . . . . a book, a shoe, an ID card. Hold these objects until you get your pen back. Students love this.

Supply safari—unsnafued

Your spritely friend never has books or pencils when he needs them. Sit down and make a list with him. If students are allowed to go to lockers three times a day, divide list in three.

First Trip	Second Trip	Third Trip
1. Speller	1. Music instrument	1. Art project
2. Notebook, compass, pen	2. Flash cards	2. Smock
3. Math workbook and text	3. Reader	3. Library book
4. Gym shoes	4. Lunch	4. Etc.

Tape one copy of this list inside his desk and another inside his locker.

Hand me sunglasses, please

When, against your warnings, a youngster persists in using wildly colored ink for assignments, don't scold. Tell him in mock exaggeration that the colored ink so hurts your eyes you can't even look at his paper, let alone grade it.

No wax tablet or stylus, either

No pencil or paper, again? Don't fret, friendly teacher. Don't nag, either. Sell them needed paper: two sheets for 1¢; pens rent for 1¢ a period. Let them borrow from a classmate if they've no cash, or let them run a credit account. Students enjoy this arrangement very much. Evidently paying money removes an implied need to be grateful for a personal favor. It's a good intermediate step between buying paper ahead of time and depending on dole in class.

PAPERS WITHOUT NAMES

This perennial annoyance can be eliminated pleasantly. Teaching a forgetful child to sign his papers is actually reminding him that considerations and courtesy are a two-way street. He learns to be mindful of a teacher's problems—in this case the huge stack of papers she must go through. This lesson also helps him realize he is one more member of a group.

Most teachers first warn the children, and then either accommodate them by learning individual handwriting, or discomfit them by discarding unsigned papers. Here are several in-between steps.

Johnny has an alias

Choose a famous name . . . Peter Cottontail, Paul Revere, Willie Mays, Peanuts, and put it on the child's paper in felt marker printing. Never again will he forget to sign his work. The surprise has a shock effect. This technique is good for any age level.

After you sign your name

Distribute papers. Ask children to place their names on their papers. After they've done this, they are to stand and hold the papers under their chins. Lower grades.

The hardest working monkey in town

Hang a large, stuffed monkey on a bulletin board and let children choose a name. When you get an unsigned paper, put the monkey's name on it. A good unsigned paper is posted on bulletin board; a poor one is put in a desk drawer. If a child doesn't get his paper back, he knows where to look.

Over and over and over . . . and over

First time, warn forgetful child. Second time, have him sign his papers twice. If he forgets again, increase number of signatures to five, ten or 20.

Everyday in the same way

A uniform position for the student's name on all papers is helpful. In other words, avoid having him put his name in the upper right hand for one lesson and on the bottom for the next.

INCOMPLETE WORK

A habit of incompleteness is a state of thinking. It should be corrected in a child's outlook as well as in his assignments. Usually, all his activities suffer; rare is the child who does only a half a job on his schoolwork and yet finishes other projects. Learning to budget time in work and play, and practicing stick-to-itiveness, are required.

Every time there's a glimmer of increased perseverence, laud it. If he finishes a task, no matter how messily, don't make him redo it. Firmly establish a pattern of completing jobs. Later on, tackle teaching him tidier habits—pride in a job not only done, but well done.

As teacher, you set a pace. If you find incomplete work widespread in your room, look around at your own projects. Set target dates for finishing pet extras. By that date, do them or drop them entirely.

Several teachers suggested these. If this habit isn't broken in a reasonably short time, delve deeper into causes.

Play early–pay later

This style of form letter is an aid when it is necessary to send work home. It helps avoid scolding during school hours.

Date ____________________

Dear ____________________,

I talked and played in school and disturbed others. Now I am to do my work during my play time.

Signed ____________________

Parent's signature ____________________

Three day limit

Strangely, a normal student turns in almost no work, or very poor work, three days in a row. Tell him you plan to call home. Put your call through. Ask his mother if there is anything at school or home which is troubling her child. Then report the unsatisfactory progress of the week.

MESSY WORK

Try writing with your toes. You'll relearn a fact: learning to write is hard work. Probably you won't stay with your efforts long enough to acquire a Palmer stroke, but you'll grow in your desire to be gentle with your little ham fisted students.

If your district has a standards manual for English, get it out. Read the points you plan to stress to the children. No longer will they be a pet idiosyncrasy of yours; the book makes it impersonal. No matter what you think of these rules, these children are going to have to live with them all their school years. Even if, or especially if, you think some of the rules are fussy, consider the fact that you'll be doing the child a favor if you teach him these.

This is preferable to letting him learn them from a teacher who thinks the rules are so important, that she chops down his well earned grades on subject matter.

One day, when speaking to them about neat work, explain the term "halo effect" and its impact on teachers. Show them concrete examples of how general appearance doesn't affect the impact of the thoughts presented, but it does affect grades.

In trying to teach neatness it's easy to fall back on a child's desire to please his teacher, this year's boss in his eyes. Yet learning simple, non-commital ways of pleasing one's boss is good preparation for successful living at any age. It actually strengthens a child for he has established himself as a co-operative person in reputation; therefore, when he speaks up and out on matters which count, people will listen. He hasn't labelled himself as a picayune obstructionist.

Here are some steps kind and earnest teachers suggested to help children overcome the crippling appearance of sloppiness.

Quicker, too

Children *can* cross out mistakes with one line. If a child deletes mistakes with many scratches, grade the paper, but don't give him credit until he copies it.

Look teach, no rule mark

An even margin, and no trace of a pencil line on the paper. Take a second sheet, fold an edge the width of the wanted margin–one or one and a half inches. Fit writing sheet into the fold. Voila! A guide line.

Note: Often with slow or discouraged students a teacher taking the time to teach them features of neatness has the warm encouragement of convincing them that they can accomplish and that they're worthy of her time.

Two margins, please

If your style manual calls for a right hand margin, try this device for students who ignore leaving a space. Warn him a few times. Then, take a felt marker and a ruler, and dramatize with a colored line down his page. You have cast yourself in the role of "Scrooge" but at the same time he'll learn the lesson–and no resentment.

Two grades on every spelling test

Put both a spelling grade and a penmanship/neatness grade on every spelling test. Use a standardized handwriting guide sheet for evaluation. You might consider using this double grade on science and social studies papers, too.

Pride can come after a fall

Tell a few students who have turned in mediocre work that you're thinking of displaying the assignment. You're considering mounting their work, too. Don't ask them to redo the papers even though their work is messy. Ask them, "Your ideas are good, do you think your friends will notice the blotches and scratches?" Invariably, students willingly and gratefully redo the papers.

Call the game "ouch"

Neater, faster penmanship is your goal. Lesson time limit: 15 minutes. Distribute four sheets of school paper and a penmanship book to each student. Choose one of two check points from the following: holding pen properly, sitting straight, digging in paper, drawing letters—any combination of these. Put chosen points on board.

Start class on a routine assignment. As you see a child fall into an error of the day, call his name. He must start over on the next sheet of paper. If he's far down the first sheet, he'll give you a pained expression. Those pained looks inspired the name of the game. Children love this lesson.

MAKE-UP WORK

Make-up work is more important than the work made up. Every day on which a child misses school brings a continuity gap. He may not have missed much, but he doesn't know it, and he fears that unknown quantity. He doesn't know where or how to ask about it. For the sake of his self-confidence, it's wise to hold him to most class work missed—in one form or another. It's as important for bright children as for average or slower ones to know that they know. Of course, your reputation for fairness is enhanced when everyone makes up missed assignments.

Departmental classes force taking class time to check with students on back assignments and tests. While this is going on, please give the class something interesting to do. Perhaps a ditto sheet on unexpected, special material. Give directions for the sheet and announce due time. Usually the freshness stimulates greater intensity of diligence than a familiar textbook assignment.

LACK OF STUDY FOR DISCUSSIONS AND TESTS

Ever since the great flood some good natured youngsters have been riding through school with as little work as possible and doing it with a *mañana* casualness. Basically, most of these students are not hostile, lazy, sly—they're human. But, no one needs to mention to you that when this condition is in its contagious stage, it virtually eliminates preparatory study, and discussions are worthless.

Using any of the following ideas for bolstering student efforts has a great advantage in that you, as teacher, need not utter one scolding word. (Excuse me, teachers exhort . . . they don't scold, do they?) Why not try some of these approaches a few times? Normally, you'll see a real change. And, if you don't see improvement, check other factors.

Steps leading up to . . . . . .

Use ditto sheets of sentences, paragraphs, numbers or statistics on the material studied. Leave key words blank. Ask your students to fill in about 2/3 before class, any 2/3 of the questions and blanks. Tell them you don't want them to fret or lose sleep on anything they find extremely difficult.

As they arrive in class, immediately give them a ✓/o grade on having 2/3 of sheet done. Students who worked seriously appreciate your doing this. Then go over the sheet orally with the group. The combination of some work beforehand, reading aloud, contributing answers and writing, produces an atmosphere they all enjoy.

There's a long, long list awaiting

Judged by past performance, the class will not know a thing about today's work. Make up and ditto a list of terms and definitions, leaving space after each entry for students to write in. Ask class to choose two or three terms and think about them briefly. Next, rotating the order around the room, *let each student select the term he wants to explain or define.* Selecting them at random keeps a surprise element. Allowing him to choose lets him put his best foot forward. You'll gain his gratitude as well as fewer wrong answers. This is not a deep learning process, but it will help to shake a group out of a "gather ye rosebuds while you may" outlook. And, most important, slow students really enjoy this procedure.

Science bowl

This is patterned after College Bowl and it was developed for students who refused to study for tests. CAUTION: First time, it'll be a dud. Second time, it'll be a success. Later times, it'll be so successful and the children will try so hard, you'll get an accurate picture of how much they know without giving the test.

Example: Divide room into two groups. Each child writes five questions relating to the study unit, and puts answers on back of paper. He may write more if he desires, and many do. During the game ask question once. If you don't get a correct answer, go on to the next question. In a Lightning Round, pick up all questions children missed earlier. In this last round, if a child pauses in middle of an answer, someone else on his team may complete it.

Surface diving–then depth

Your class keeps coming without having studied. When you prepare your thoughtful discussion questions, zero in on specific objective points or data. Next, make up a surprise quiz on the specifics–hard, but not sneaky hard. Ditto it and distribute to class on their arrival. Ask them to take the test, exchange papers, and grade. They will do badly.

Next stage. Remind class that your first concern is their learning; therefore if, as a group, they can pool enough ideas and facts on the coming discussion questions, or if they ask stimulating questions of each other so that a good thing gets rolling, you'll not record the quiz grades. During the ensuing discussion you'll notice a shift of effort–you won't be trying to pull out responses, the students will be offering information and trying to do their share.

Hand outs

You're quite sure no one will arrive prepared for today. Using a different question for each class member, put one question on a sheet of paper. Have each person answer a question without using the text and then have him pass his paper to a friend or classmate. This friend is to write a good answer using the text. Sometimes, have youngster grade these, other times not. In any case, return papers to the original writers and allow class a few minutes for chatter among themselves. You'll hear, "What one did she hand you? Listen to the one I got. What's wrong with this answer?"

Party of the first part asks

And party of the second part answers. Ask each student to put his name on two sheets of paper. Next, ask class to take a few minutes and compose three good quiz questions on the day's assignment, open book. On the second sheet of paper they are to write good, normal answers to the three questions. They are to keep the answer sheets and turn question sheets in to you. You redistribute. The second student writes answers. At a deadline time, have each student give his answer to the author who shall grade it by comparison with his own answer. He will then return graded paper and his own answer to the quiz taker. Collect papers. Normally don't record grades, at least the first time or two.

These techniques could be described as pump-priming. As you continue to rouse interest with techniques like these, you'll find a few more students coming prepared each day. For times when the class is reviewing for a test, there are effective approaches.

CHEATING

A child who cheats needs help. Regardless of how you handle the immediate situation, the long term solution is to see he gets help. And handle the immediate situation you must—the other children need affirmation of your basic fairness.

In talking with the errant child, explain that cheating is a sign of weakness. You want him to develop or to show strength. He may need help in learning how to study more efficiently. Or he may have a subject mastery and only lack self-confidence. A third possibility may be his tendency to be a leaner.

After you've caught him and he has paid the price, forget it. Almost, anyway. When the occasion arises, put him in a position where he can show his trustworthiness. Commend him when he lives up to your restored trust in him.

Here are some immediate correctional steps which considerate teachers have offered:

Credit where credit is due

If you see a child copying during a test, have him put the child's name after the answer he copied. Author's note: This seems an especially humane and courteous way of handling cheating. It alerts him to the fact that you caught him but the sanction is mild enough to be appropriate.

Co-operation during exams is called cheating

And the solution is simple. Stand in rear of room during testing hour. Either students' laxity or your suspicions will disappear. If child raises his hand, have him come to you: don't you leave your post.

Plagiarism

First offense: A one-to-one talk. Ask student to redo report, in his own words, by the next morning. Lower his grade one notch. Second offense: A one-to-one talk. Grade paper F. Ask student to do another report on another subject and have it in the next morning. Third offense: Automatic and final F.

CONCLUSION

In this chapter we've taken up a few facets of study and work-habit improvement, to help poor students into mediocrity and mediocre students into excellence. The basic qualities of thinking for good students are: perception, reason, memory, application and judgment. Every student in school can work on these in some fashion. Then there's a call for orderly, coherent and unified actions, first in the larger elements of the students' experience and then in the details.

Measuring results is a precious activity to educators. Alas, work and study habit improvement won't provide an attractive statistic sheet. Children like to measure results, too. They like rewards for their efforts–while they're still children. Therefore, if your class learns a procedure or two well, take an educated guess at the time saved. Give them a fun lesson in that time, and tell them they've earned it by their co-operation and aptness as pupils.

11 Excursions Inside the Building--To the Library Resource Center, and Assembly

Nihil est . . . simul et inventum et perfectum.
(Nothing is both discovered and perfected at the same time.)

-Cicero

Since this chapter deals mainly with guiding children's conduct while they are enjoying the modern enrichments many schools provide, it seemed appropriate to start with a rich, traditional touch of Latin. As you know, many classroom teachers across the nation are called on to be once a week librarians or fortnightly assembly supervisors. Normally these teachers have reasonable order in the school room, but sometimes youngsters can be a little bucky outside their native habitat. Here is some information offered by interviewed teachers. I hope it will help other teachers to use a soft and sure touch in managing children on their building excursions.

The first section, on libraries and resource centers, starts with a few suggestions teachers gave me about enrichment reading in the classroom. Next are presented rules from a few library and resource center personnel. These provide an idea base from which to adapt new, tailor-made guidelines for other situations. Following this, we will discuss a few suggestions on methods of paying for lost or stolen property, and for defacement of materials. (Also see Chapter 4.)

The second section takes up aspects of preventative and corrective measures which relate to troublesome student conduct in assembly.

HOMEROOM LIBRARY: HAPPINESS TIME

The primary purpose of this book is to help teachers in their responsibility for self-disciplined students. The following suggestions are included because of their morale-building features. The teachers who offered them are highly successful in developing happy, harder-working students.

Children need the self-respect and strength which come from adding to the well-being of others. This project below has been especially successful in poor neighborhoods. The obvious shortage of books is one factor, but only one factor. A dearth of material possessions causes many people to forget the need everyone has, the poor included, to reap the satisfaction of being able to give.

Even Carnegie started with only a dime

Students may fund this library from their allowances or from doing chores. As teacher, you may match the total—no more. It is important to avoid taking parental dollars. After accumulating some money, one adult and several students form a committee and choose and buy books. Since this won't take much of the adults'

Name____________________

Title____________________

Author____________________

What is the book about?____________________

The part I like best____________________

Instructions to student: After you've completed this side, add on the back a pen, pencil or crayon sketch of the part you like best.

time, the children might enjoy working with a well-liked speech or gym teacher. The pilot committee sets up the necessary rules, too.

Book reports–out of print

Poor or rich, skinny or fat, wee or tall, children rarely enjoy writing book reports. This drudgery can be circumvented in many imaginative ways. Taping, puppets, pictures, etc. I have included only one, a not-particularly imaginative but very good dittoed form. It's a fine intermediate position between the old-style book report and the temptations which come from merely asking students to list on a card the titles of books which they've read.

Just before temptation ......

If your class gets a bad library conduct report, make your scolding short. Save your breath. Just prior to their next library visit have a discussion and role playing session. Seat a few pupils around a table and have them choose books, read, and turn pages. Save one chair. As children are demonstrating purposeful conduct, have a trouble-making clown sit in the empty seat and start disrupting everyone. Follow his performance with another short discussion. Sometimes let a second group play these roles.

LIBRARY AND RESOURCE CENTER

Many studies have shown that initiative and curiosity seem to be stifled somehow during the middle years of elementary schooling. This gradual intellectual atrophy can be reversed when children work with congenial agemates in the stimulating atmosphere of new devices and fascinating, fresh topics of a good resource center.

On occasions you probably send an individual or pairs of students to the center to work. You'll sense which students need a modicum of directional goals. The following form, filled out in duplicate, makes a good map. You can keep one copy and the other copy goes to the center's attendant. Just your filling out a form helps the student focus his attention and reminds him impersonally and without scolding that he's going there to discover, search for answers and work.

RESOURCE LEARNING CENTER

Name ______________________ Teacher ______________________

Date ______________ Time ______________to______________

Prescribed Activity	Self-Selected Activity
Reading ____________ Level ____________	
Math ______________ Level ____________	
Science Topic ______________	Science Topic ______________
Social Studies ______________	Social Studies ______________
Creative Writing ____________	Creative Writing ____________
Art ________________________	Art ________________________
Other ______________________	Other ______________________

Suggested Material or Equipment ______________________________

____

The Day They Let a Classroom Teacher be Librarian

Everyone tells you: Be firm in controls and relax them gradually as students prove themselves and a good atmosphere has been set. There are sound reasons for this advice. Children find security within a sturdy framework of rules considerately administered. When a child has learned what is expected of him in behavior, he is free to proceed to other forms of learning. Definite procedures help you to be more consistent in adhering to standards.

Whether you are in a library full-time, or take your class occasionally, you need guidelines. After a while you can make intelligent exceptions in individual cases. Here are some good basic rules:

1. Ask students to sit three to a six-chair table, four to an eight-chair table, and in alternate chairs at a round table. With a smiling voice tell them of your great concern-they must have lots of room for their books.
2. Friends may sit with friends until they prove they can't handle the privilege.
3. Special permission is required if more than a specified number want to sit at a table.

4. Immediately on entering library, students take their seats.
5. Make necessary announcements.
6. Personally extend permission to go to shelves.
7. Warning call a few minutes before bell. All books must be signed out or taken back to shelf. Return to seats.
8. Dismissal.

Seating diagram for library

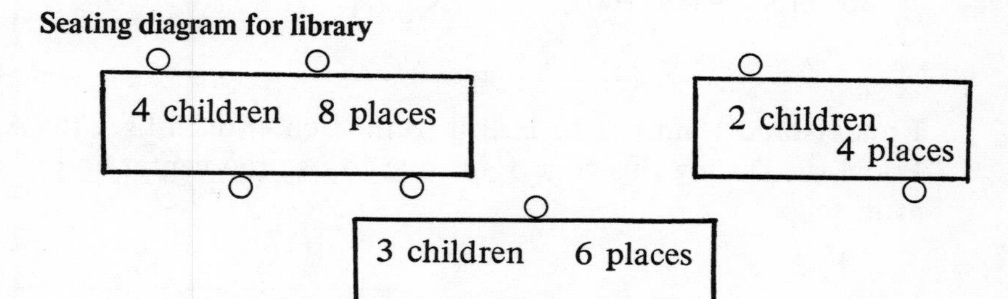

A few here . . . a few there

Parcel out the children to various tables as they come through the door. "Sylvester, over here . . . Lester, near the window, Ann, over there . . . Elizabeth, near the display, please."

Don't slam the door as you leave

Sometimes the politest, simplest move you can make is to hand talking students a *Disciplinary Pass.* Already they know they've been breaking rules.

Disciplinary Pass

Your talking is excessive.
Therefore, you are NOT TO RETURN to the Center TODAY.
This is a pass to ______________________

Multilateral pact

This form is useful when it is necessary to dismiss a badly misbehaving student. Asking him for his signature has a salutary effect. Along with this add a few brief, appropriate comments.

(Student's last name, first name) Date ______________

The above named student was asked to leave the RC because (s)he was not making proper use of the center.

ID attached ______________

____
Signature – RC Staff

No ID ______________

____

I understand I am not to return to the Center until I see the Ass't Principal. During this time I am free to use the center before and after school.

____
Student Signature

____

____
Student's Last Name, First Name

Indicate status of student:

____
Assistant Principal

Administrator: Please return lower portion of form to RC

Have we made ourselves clear?

One resource center was having difficulty putting over the fact to the students that the main purpose of the center was learning, not socializing activity. The staff then issued the following bulletin:

Resource Center Rules

The center is divided into two areas—an area of quiet talking and an area of silent individual study. "Quiet talking" means that students may talk with each other about school work while they are seated at the tables in that area along the east side of the center. "Silent individual study" means there is no talking of any kind between students. The larger part of the Center is set aside for this purpose. Students are simply not to speak unless it is to a teacher or a member of the Resource Center staff. Talking by one student to another in this area including before and after school (and during passing periods) will result in a student being assigned a dentention. Boundaries of the two areas are carefully marked.

If, in the judgment of a teacher or the RC staff, a student is abusing the quiet study area, or if a student is talking in the silent, individual study area, he will be assigned a dentention to be served the same day. If the student is uncooperative, a misconduct report will be written.

The Resource Center, its staff, and the teaching staff are present to serve student needs, to provide students with services and an environment appropriate to serious study and individual accomplishment. It is hoped that students will make this facility a real center of learning and teacher-student interaction. Students should always ask staff members for help when assistance is needed in locating materials.

ASSEMBLY

The youngsters are agog! Today, there's an all-school assembly. Training your class for this event calls for preparing them, getting them seated in the auditorium, and then making provision for the few jokers who act up. Of course, the best deterrent for mischievous behavior is a good program; but, as you well know, sometimes you and the class are just stuck.

As I interviewed teachers on the topic of conduct at assembly, they offered to share the following suggestions.

There's one or two in every crowd

Prepare the children for assembly hall programs with role-playing. Ask five or six children to come to the front of the room and demonstrate good audience demeanor, for an assembly or anywhere. Then instruct two more to join the group—let these characters do everything they shouldn't. Follow this impromptu theatrical with a discussion by the whole group. A timely scheduling of this lesson would be just before an assembly.

Forearmed is forewarned

Prepare the children for a school assembly with a pep talk. Then give explicit directions on the conduct expected of them. Perhaps write something similar to the following rules on the board. Elicit many of the ideas from the students.

1. Act like graders. [We/you have earned this status, show it.]
2. No talking. [No need, we/you've been together all morning.]
3. No scuffling or fooling around.
4. Don't touch anyone else's legs or feet.
5. Stay alert.
6. Obey another teacher without argument. [If you object to her directions, you are to obey her and discuss it with me later.]
7. One punishment brings another. [If another teacher needs to punish a member of this class, he may expect another punishment from me later because his antics have detracted from the room's reputation.]

May I walk you to assembly?

Eighth grade boys escort the girls. Thus walking in pairs, no formal line is needed. The teacher initiates the selecting by calling a boy's name. He in turn asks a girl. If the teacher will choose the socially non-glamorous boys first, they tend to choose the mousier girls. As a result the occasion does not become a social barometer. At first a teacher may hear reluctant remarks and get a resistence, but if she observes carefully, she will find it is on the surface only.

Boy . . . girl . . . boy . . . girl

Clusters of boys sitting together are easily tempted into horseplay. Direct the studens in the classroom into two lines, boys and girls. Let them walk to the assembly. As they are about to be seated, alternate boy, girl, boy, girl.

Miss argue, no, miss argus

The children know you have only two eyes but, if you sit in back of them in assembly, they're never quite sure when one of those eyes is taking in a sneaky antic of theirs.

Next time, bring a cushion

Warn nuisance-making student twice. With the third warning have him sit on the floor next to your seat during the program. Later, have a brief talk with him, privately.

Discipline class meets during assembly

The children from various classrooms, who have lost the privilege of viewing an assembly because of misconduct, are sent to a common room for the remaining time of the program. Here they may have group discussions on how all of organized society must have rules and why. They may be asked to do research or they may be asked to sit and meditate on the error of their ways. Needless to add, some adult in the building must be in charge.

CONCLUSION

The brief material on library periods, resource center rules and assembly conduct was included because, though these activities take little weekly time, they're the frosting of the schedule, breaks in the routine, and they should be affable and especially relaxed—without going to pieces. A very good time to discuss conduct requirements for these events is before the fact, not after.

The model plans and rules offered are particularly intended for helping the classroom teacher who occasionally takes her group on building excursions. Knowing the type of rules and methods which others have established for their groups would help a teacher make wise adaptations for her own class.

12 Rapport with the Home

In his book *Autocrat of the Breakfast Table* Oliver Wendell Holmes remarks, "Scientific knowledge, even in the most modest persons, has mingled with it a something which partakes of insolence. Absolute peremptory facts are bullies, and those who keep company with them are apt to get a bullying frame of mind."

Since she is armed with test scores and statistics on behavior patterns, the well-trained teacher should be especially alert to this danger. She should guard against unwittingly seeming to promote her views with too much of that "something"—especially when dealing with parents.

Such a weakness could be corrected by a teacher showing sincere respect for parental feelings. Members of other professions thrive or fail according to the number of clients they attract. In varying degree the state still decides which school a child shall attend; but a wise teacher takes the trouble to ensure that parents understand her and value her services. Then—ideally—if the parents had free choice, they would still choose her to teach their child.

Harmony in human affairs is built in part on mutually agreeable relationships and charitable good will. Moreover, true charity does not overlook errors, or make semi-valid, conjectural excuses for them—only false charity does that.

Any sensitive teacher can listen carefully when a parent speaks, not only to the words he is uttering or muttering, but for the underlying values and trends he's holding in esteem. Somewhere viewpoints are bound to coincide; and, many or few, these points make the only valid starting base.

Basic security is essential regardless of whether a youngster's parents agree with you or not, please don't be afraid of cramping any child's creativity by insisting on a reasonable atmosphere in the classroom. Chaos always breeds insecurity, which in turn paralyzes creativity. Creativity requires self-control and a sense of self-discipline which knows when to conform and when to refuse to conform, but re-reserves the right for each individual to be his own judge and jury in creative efforts. Freedom in the air, enveloping a basic feeling of security and stability, establishes the atmosphere needed to nurture sound individualism in adults and children.

Frequently parents ask, "What can I do to best help my child become a better student, to be more successful?" One's thought instinctively flashes to a good lamp, a dictionary, and a quiet corner. Far more vital in promoting a child's progress are the home's attitudes toward the genuine value of education. It may be necessary to remind a parent that the greatest encouragement to a child is recognized success of his school work, work already complete. Incidentally, many educators feel there is no greater deterrent to classroom misbehavior than a student's enjoyment of his own recognized success in his studies.

Some parents unwisely criticize a child's school or teachers in his presence. This erodes his respect for some or all concerned, divides his loyalties, hobbles his progress. Occasionally harmony may be restored by reminding parents that a child is encouraged and reassured by a feeling of oneness of educational purpose between house and classroom. Suggest that you have tried to eliminate hair-splitting criticisms of students—if you have. If not, eliminate them. Then, (if necessary) gently ask the parent to examine his motives carefully and weigh the importance of his comments to actually improving conditions. Thus he could probably eliminate carping criticism and nit picking at the staff and curriculum . . . and confine his complaints to matters which really count. And make them privately to the school, not to his child. This doesn't mean pretending that whatever the school does is right; and certainly you'll be glad to talk things over with parents who feel at serious variance with you. Petty criticism acts like termites, silently undermining until suddenly someone's foot goes through the floor.

Thirdly, how about reminding a parent of the power of his own good example of specific qualities and traits? Suggest to him that he make a concerted effort at expressing in all of his daily activities the very qualities which he sees as weak in the child—be the qualities alertness, remembering, diligence, completing tasks. The effects will rub off. And so, if both parents earnestly exemplify the traits which need strengthening in the youngster, the child is sure to be strengthened. One aside—anyone working hard to improve a weakness of his own is not prone to nagging others for the same failing.

INFORMAL CONTACTS WITH THE HOME

An excellent way of building innate understanding with parents is to call at the child's home and discuss his progress, without waiting until an incident triggers the visit. Telephone first to arrange the visit. Generally you'll feel a grateful welcome, especially in more humble homes. Frequently you'll acquire many insights in a few minutes, because parents are natural and relaxed.

At troubled times in school consider making a casual phone call to a parent. Usually, it's most appreciated. Let's say a child suddenly acts up in school. A call home may quickly uncover a contributory difficulty. Gracefully approach the question by asking, "Is there anything at school which is bothering Sylvester?" Once in a while you'll learn of a snag at school: but most often a parent will volunteer information of a home turmoil. Then you can act accordingly, and the parent will be alerted to how deeply affected the child is.

And speaking of affecting people deeply, try calling the parents when young John does unusually well on a particular project or test. It's extremely thoughtful and considerate, and parents will love you for it. Mom can greet Daddy with, "there's good news this very day—"

Here are some other bridges and routes which practicing teachers have used with marked success:

For information dial . . . .

The student's home phone number. Most teachers, particularly inner city teachers, who have called each student's home serveral times a semester, enthusiastically report excellent results. Calls are an outstanding way of establishing strong relationships and good feeling. In half an hour satisfying calls with about five homes are possible. Avoid alphabetizing or timing patterns for calls. Judgment day can thus come anytime in a student's life, so he must keep himself in a state of comparative grace most of the time.

Instead of ex post facto

One foresighted way to keep good feeling with the home is to send out—about half way through the quarter—a progress letter. This should be early enough in the marking period to enable a child and his family to do something to boost a poor or mediocre grade.

Date ____________________

Dear ____________________,

Thus far this quarter we have taken ________ quizzes.

Specifically, ________________ got quiz grades of ________. ________, ________, ________, and ________. Therefor his present grade is approximately a/an ________.

His grade is not final and is subject to change before or by the end of this quarter. In case this midquarter grade is unsatisfactory, there is still sufficient time to bring it up to an acceptable level.

Cordially your,

Ben Gillies
Mathematics Instructor

Parents Comments ______________________________
____
____
____

. . . . "If you don't get a letter . . . "

Parents need facts if they're going to co-operate wisely. A form letter sent weekly can be most effective. You might initiate the system with an introductory letter and continue it with a weekly model.

Sample Introductory Letter

VERY GOOD SATISFACTORY IMPROVEMENT NEEDED
UNSATISFACTORY

Dear Parents,

We both realize that a good attitude is often the key to academic success. This year we plan to offer your child a wide variety of learning experiences. But all our plans are wasted unless your child is constantly encouraged to develop self-control. Thus we intend to ask your cooperation in our efforts toward fostering self-discipline.

Each Friday your child will bring home a deportment slip. If he has "very good" he has excelled in self-control. "Good" indicates a positive effort made by your child. "Improvement needed" indicates a lack of effort on your child's part. The last mark, "unsatisfactory," reflects a definite disregard for self-discipline.

Please sign this first deportment letter and have your child return it Monday. Thank you for your cooperation.

Sincerely yours,

Mrs. Elizabeth Arras

Sample Weekly Letter

VERY GOOD SATISFACTORY IMPROVEMENT NEEDED UNSATISFACTORY

Dear Parents,

The above circled word indicates the conduct of your child for this week. "Very good" or satisfactory indicates a definite progress in your child's conduct. "Improvement needed" indicates a definite lack of self-control. An "unsatisfactory" mark shows that your child's work this week has been greatly effected by his poor behavior in class. You need not sign this paper unless your child has received an "unsatisfactory" mark.

Sincerely yours,

Date Mrs. Elizabeth Arras

Challenging the lack of change

Three of the above letters marked "unsatisfactory" bring a conference attended by the child, teacher, principal and *both* parents. When the family wage-earner has to rearrange his affairs in order to come to school, it alerts him to the seriousness of his responsibility for his child's schooling.

One successful and ambitious teacher has developed this form letter. When he sends one of these home, he tries always to mark either positive comments alone or both positive and negative comments if his primary concern is correction.

Dear Parents:

I would like to inform you when your child has done something outstanding at school or has made some progress overcoming a problem. On the other hand, I believe you should also be aware when your child is not conforming to school regulations.

In order to do this the following check list will serve for this purpose. It will include a check list, a place for comment for either the teacher or parent and a place for the parent to sign and return the slip to school. A repeated negative occurence will be followed up with a phone call and on the third occasion either or both parents will be asked to come to school.

Outstanding Accomplishment or Progress Solving a Problem	**Not Following Rules**
School Grounds:	*School Grounds:*
Careful on playground	Running
Is careful of others	Pushing
Getting along well	Fighting
Does not throw snowballs	Throwing snowballs
Uses equipment carefully	Improper use of equipment
Halls:	*Halls:*
Walks carefully in hall	Running
Is quiet in hall	Making noies
Goes directly to destination	Not going directly to destination
Enters building when bell rings	Entering building before bell
Classroom:	*Classroom:*
Completing work carefully	Disturbing others
Working quietly	Working carelessly
Showed special interest	Not completing work

Lunchroom:	*Lunchroom:*
Speaks in soft voice	Causing a disturbance
Does not disturb others	Leaving supervised area
Obeys person in charge	
Does not leave supervised area	
Other:	*Other:*

COMMENTS:

Parent's signature____________________

PARENT CONFERENCES

Most teachers view conferences with one clear, sparkling eye and one jaundiced eye. Probably the faculty has a slight edge on parents in enjoying Open House, although most parents would agree they need conference night more than the teacher does. If a teacher has a mild problem student, she has access to many avenues of help and advice; however, if a parent is beseiged with doubts over a minor problem, or if he wants to check his progress as a parent when all is relatively normal at home—there's no place he can go. Hence, many parents regard school conferences as a barometer of their own success.

Understanding this fact, we can see why most parents may be a little ill at ease under their poised bearing and casual questions. Since they're coming to our fire for the pow wow, it is up to us to light the peace pipe of friendliness. Welcome them warmly. (One teacher was so cordial she even served homemade cookies and brewed coffee on parents' night. A tremendous hit.) Sharing even the lightest refreshments always seems to promote fellowship. (If you try something like this, you'd probably be smart to get advance clearance from the office. The janitors in your building might have an anti-cookie-crumb clause in their contract.)

Curiously, in widely separated schools, several teachers with urbane manners offered some identical points as the most important in setting a right tone. Foremost, they said, if you really feel you and the parents are partners, sit around a table as equals. Or even at a two student desk, IF THE PARENT FITS COMFORTABLY. These very professional teachers did concede that an insecure teacher might need the prop of her desk and books. Another exception might be in meeting with a blood-in-his-eye parent—then, sometimes, it's wise for a teacher to keep a professional desk between the parent and herself.

Nevertheless, most conferences would be at a table. And to promote casualness, the interviewed teachers emphasized having no official records on this table, not even a grade book. The child's card and folder should easily be available but not visible, at least during the initial stages of the meeting. And, please avoid writing anything in front of the parent. If you simply must jot down memos, invite your guest to do likewise and offer him a card and a pencil. Most important, of course, is your friendly spirit . . . . all the mechanics mean nothing without that.

In order to turn on a parent's fluency, one polished English teacher, a Mr. Gearing, explained his approach. He starts by posing a question, "How is Bobbie doing in English?" The startled parent responds, "Ye gods, you're the English teacher. You're asking me?" Then Mr. Gearing explains that surely he knows what's going on in class, but he's interested in what the child is carrying home. From then on, usually, the parent begins divulging information.

If Bobbie likes the class, the parent usually offers positive remarks or recalls incidents the child has mentioned. Parental hesitancy often indicates that the child doesn't like English this year. Then clarifying questioning is needed to expose the roots of the dislike. Sometimes a parent says, "I don't know how Bobbie feels about English, He doesn't tell me much about any of his subjects." Naturally, Mr. Gearing delicately delves into the reasons for the conversation breakdown at home.

Another way a teacher sets the tone is by opening with a remark such as "Bruce is having trouble in English," and then waiting for a parental expression or explanation. While making such a statement, voice inflexion is of paramount importance. Let it be gentle, friendly, patient.

A rejoicing parent! When, during fall open house, a departmental teacher recalls a moment or earmark which indirectly proves she knows the child as an individual, a parent is shocked, happily so. You could even make a crib including names and unique features . . . . the title of a foolish poem the child likes, his puppy's name, his druthers on almost anything. Once you've prepared your list you probably won't have to refer to it; you'll remember.

There comes the time when you must ask for a special conference, an unhappy one. Several outstanding teachers advised me they consider the following moves important: After preliminary discussion with parents, 1) offer one or two constructive steps for the home to take. It seems wiser to offer a limited number of ideas rather than risk overwhelming the parent. Also, 2) inform the parent of what you plan to do. Then, 3) *offer* to phone a month later with a progress report. If parents agree, immediately mark the phoning date on your calendar. Finally, 4) as you phone on the promised day you'll hear a mother thrilled with your attitude and sense of professional responsibility. Now, if not before, she realizes that you do indeed care.

Several very tactful teachers suggested the following points as having contributed to their own successful meetings with parents:

Ask, don't wait to be told

Take the initiative and ask parent, "Is any child in the room making your child uncomfortable?" Often a mild situation exists which the parent hesitates to report. If you are aware of a difficulty, you can act in several quiet ways to help both children.

Positive, negative, positive

Always start the appointment with a positive comment about little Charley. For every negative point please be sure to suggest a remedy or a constructive step to try. Finally, save at least one garland of praise for the child, to end the interview with.

. . . . Balanced scales of justice

Work for spending an equal amount of time on negative and positive notes in your visits with parents.

Co-sponsor a specific point

Elicit from parents *their* plans to help Archibald, Jr., this year. If there are key weaknesses on which they plan to work, you may be able to join the home program by stressing the same points at school.

Every day can be parent conference day

During a conference mention that you are always as close as the telephone. Give them your number. Invite them to call. Parents do not abuse this invitation. Parents lacking much formal education are especially appreciative, since many of them have never outgrown a timidity in talking to teachers. As an added dividend, children lose the temptation to work one side, the home, against the other, the school.

Best foot forward

On conference night leave several magazines on chairs outside your door. Among them place some professional periodicals. Since your parent guests are not likely to have seen these issues before, they'll find some articles interesting. Also, the publications serve as a tactful reminder that teaching is a profession, and that your judgments comes as a result of your professional training, not just of your personality.

Teaching has changed: results should, too.

One growing-point which a parent welcomes when he stops to think it over is: "Don't limit your offspring by your experiences in school." The math-was-always-hard-for-me outlook of an adult, though sympathetically intended, actually deprives a youngster of an obligation to make a genuine effort. Often, it introduces a hurdle before he gets into the race. Math may have been hard for the parent because he missed some basics, or because his teachers taught with little clarity or sparkle, not because of his aptitude deficiency. Or the teaching itself may have been excellent and the parent bound by the heredity superstition of grandpa's math-was-always-hard-for-me outlook.

Let him fiddle with a timer, too.

Frequently parents of slow students are confronted with the children's dawdling over homework. What can they do to overcome this and still not nag? One way: Parent and child decide together, with the child leading the decision, how much he will accomplish in 45 minutes. Then let the child set the kitchen stove timer—almost every home has one.

Do come again when you can stay longer

A good conference conclusion is to invite the parents to visit while the class is in session. Suggest they make it a long visit in order to get the feel of the room. A side note—during a short visit the child is on his best behavior; for a long visit he will lapse into his normal behavior. Consequently, on a leisurely stay the parents get an accurate picture of how Junior compares with the class.

THE LATCHSTRING IS OUT

Currently parents and teachers are visiting in groups of ten or twelve. The aim is conversation deeper than a cocktail party and yet not as intense as a one-to-one visit. The results: A much better sense of friendship, almost every time. The invited enjoy themselves, and the teachers feel their time is well spent.

Pop visits junior's office

Sack lunch for 11. Plan your guest list to include diverse types of background and outlooks, a good mix. Ask five children in your class to invite their fathers to lunch at school one day. Surprisingly, a high percentage of men are able to arrange to make this lunch date, if they have advance notice. Everyone brings his own lunch. Sometime during the noon hour let each child take his father on a tour of the building.

Saturday . . . anywhere but the matinee

The nucleus: a Saturday outing for 12 people. The place: anywhere that's fun—an airport—a dog show—a private farm—a circus. Usually pairs of teachers plan these events. Each teacher invites two parent-child combinations, and then invites a child whom she knows is short changed when it comes to parental attention. And everyone goes off in a little pack and has a great time.

Sunday evening at 7:30

A busing program inspired this series of coffees. The school PTA president is the coordinator; she with her committee planned for groups of parents to meet monthly in various homes. About ten parent members comprise the fixed membership of each group, and one or two teachers (not always the same ones) are present at each gathering. From time to time the circle views slides or movies taken at school; however, the parents' children belong to different classes, so the projection must be an all-school film. The main object of these parties is to cultivate friendly conversation with others of different racial backgrounds in a natural home setting.

CONCLUSION

In this last chapter we've discussed the importance of a teacher taking the initiative in establishing real understanding with a child's family. This move is dictated by professional ethics and the teacher's high sense of responsibility; as a staff member of the school she makes her work easier and more effective by rapport with the family; and so, as a sympathetic friend of youngsters, her influence for good is made deeper and much far reaching.

Informal contacts by spontaneous phone calls and informative letters are very much appreciated by parents. Often timidly, they yearn for more information from school, and yet they hesitate to bother a busy teacher—perhaps out of consideration for her time, and perhaps out of fear that their requests might boomerang on their child's welfare.

Almost every district has a manual on the mechanics and procedures of formal parent conferences. As I interviewed teachers I tried to supplement that type of information with examples of thoughts and actions which these teachers considered likely to add a patina to the occasion. They stressed that these conferences can best be enhanced by anticipating unvoiced questions, and then weaving comments around the things you learn from your adroit feelers.

A few teachers claim large rewards from additional socializing with the students and/or their parents in the form of a gathering of ten or twelve.

The most precious items we have in the school room today are the child's time and the teacher's time. The child's time is so incredibly valuable because these are the years which fix the set of his sails—not unalterably, but very strongly. The teacher's time is valuable on two counts; the first, the vast amount of good she can do if her time is employed at its best, and second, the cost of it in just plain dollars and cents.

Think of the countless childish dreams for the future which would not be shattered, and the countless dollars which could be better spent, if student and teacher morale could be improved by just two or three percent through more skillful human relations and better classroom control.

INDEX

D

N

O–P

Q–R

U–V–W